Cryptocurrency Insider Secrets: 2 Manuscripts - 22 Exclusive Coins Under $1 with Potential for Huge Profits in 2018

This book contains 2 manuscripts:

- Cryptocurrency: Insider Secrets - 12 Exclusive Coins Under $1 with Potential for Huge Profits in 2018
- Cryptocurrency: Insider Secrets 2 - 10 Exciting Crypto Projects Under $1 To Make You Wealthy in 2018

By Stephen Satoshi

The following eBook is reproduced below with the goal of providing information that is as accurate and reliable as possible. Regardless, purchasing this eBook can be seen as consent to the fact that both the publisher and the author of this book are in no way experts on the topics discussed within and that any recommendations or suggestions that are made herein are for entertainment purposes only. Professionals should be consulted as needed prior to undertaking any of the action endorsed herein.

This declaration is deemed fair and valid by both the American Bar Association and the Committee of Publishers Association and is legally binding throughout the United States.

Furthermore, the transmission, duplication or reproduction of any of the following work including specific information will be considered an illegal act irrespective of if it is done electronically or in print. This extends to creating a secondary or tertiary copy of the work or a recorded copy and is only allowed with express written consent from the Publisher. All additional right reserved.

The information in the following pages is broadly considered to be a truthful and accurate account of facts and as such any inattention, use or misuse of the information in question by the reader will render any resulting actions solely under their purview. There are no scenarios in which the publisher or the original author of this work can be in any fashion deemed liable for any hardship or damages that may befall them after undertaking information described herein.

Additionally, the information in the following pages is intended only for informational purposes and should thus be thought of as universal. As befitting its nature, it is presented without assurance regarding its prolonged validity or interim quality. Trademarks that are mentioned are done without written consent and can in no way be considered an endorsement from the trademark holder.

Financial Disclaimer:

I am not a financial advisor, this is not financial advice. This is not an investment guide nor investment advice. I am not recommending you buy any of the coins listed here. Any form of investment or trading is liable to lose you money.

There is no single "best" investment to be made, in cryptocurrencies or otherwise. Anyone telling you so is deceiving you.

I am not affiliated with any coin or cryptocurrency mentioned in this book.

There is no "surefire coin" - one again, anyone telling you so is deceiving you.

With many coins, especially the smaller ones, the market is liable to the spread of misinformation.

Never invest more than you are willing to lose. Cryptocurrency is not a get rich quick scheme.

Income Disclaimer:

The book may refer to business opportunities or other money-making opportunities. If any such content exists in this book, the following disclaimers apply.

You recognize and agree that we have made no implications, warranties, promises, suggestions, projections, representations or guarantees whatsoever to you about future prospects or earnings, or that you will earn any money, with respect to your purchase of books by Stephen Satoshi, and that we have not authorized any such projection, promise, or representation by others.

Any earnings or income statements, or any earnings or income examples, are only estimates of what we think you could earn. There is no assurance you will do as well as stated in any examples. If you rely upon any figures provided, you must accept the entire risk of not doing as well as the information provided. This applies whether the earnings or income examples are monetary in nature or pertain to advertising credits which may be earned (whether such credits are convertible to cash or not).

There is no assurance that any prior successes or past results as to earnings or income (whether monetary or advertising credits, whether convertible to cash or not) will apply, nor can any prior successes be used, as an indication of your future success or results from any of the information, content, or strategies. Any and all claims or representations as to income or earnings (whether monetary or advertising credits, whether convertible to cash or not) are not to be considered as "average earnings".

The Economy. The economy, both where you do business, and on a national and even worldwide scale, creates additional uncertainty and economic risk. An economic recession or depression might negatively affect the results produced by Stephen Satoshi.

Your Success Or Lack Of It. Your success in using the information or strategies provided by Stephen Satoshi depends on a variety of factors. We have no way of knowing how well you will do, as we do not know you, your background, your work ethic, your dedication, your motivation, your desire, or your business skills or practices. Therefore, we do not guarantee or imply that you will get rich, that you will do as well, or that you will have any earnings (whether monetary or advertising credits, whether convertible to cash or not), at all.

Internet businesses and earnings derived therefrom involve unknown risks and are not suitable for everyone. You may not rely on any information presented on the website or otherwise provided by us, unless you do so with the knowledge and understanding that you can experience significant losses (including, but not limited to, the loss of any monies paid to purchase books by Stephen Satoshi, and/or any monies spent setting up, operating, and/or marketing books by Stephen Satoshi, and further, that you may have no earnings at all (whether monetary or advertising credits, whether convertible to cash or not).

Affiliate Disclaimer:

Like cryptocurrency, I too believe in transparency and openness, and so I am disclosing that I've included certain products and links to those products on in this book that I will earn an affiliate commission for any purchases you make. Please note that I have not been given any free products, services or anything else by these companies in exchange for mentioning them in this book.

Accuracy Disclaimer:

All prices and market capitalizations are correct at the time of writing. Price and market cap information is sourced from coinmarketcap.com. All information in this eBook was derived from official sources where possible. Official sources meaning literature that is publicly available, provided by the development team for each cryptocurrency or company such as a company website or GitHub page. At the time of writing, some of the information is not available in English from official sources. In this case some of the information included in this eBook was obtained from unofficially translated whitepapers. Unofficially meaning either via computer translation, or third party human translation.

Contents

Cryptocurrency Insider Secrets

By Stephen Satoshi

Introduction - The state of the cryptocurrency market in 2017.

Wow, what a year it's been. Bitcoin reaching all time highs of $7,400. Ethereum skyrocketing nearly 3000% in just 9 months and even Litecoin finally broke through its 2013 barrier to hit almost $95. These are exciting times in the cryptocurrency space. And according to many market analysts, the best is yet to come.

There is a HUGE amount of hype in the cryptocurrency market right now. If you look at the Google trends data you'll see giant rises in the popularity of cryptocurrency related searches. If you look at r/cryptocurrency, the official cryptocurrency subreddit, the number of subscribers increased from 25,000 at the beginning of the year to over 134,000 at the time of writing.

Unfortunately, with this increase in popularity, there has been a significant uptick in poor information and it seems like everyday there's another heavily hyped ICO or cryptocurrency project. We've started to see ICOs advertising on social media, and using celebrity influence to try and tap into the mind of the general public. These are the types of investments I have deliberately LEFT OUT of this book. I don't want anyone investing based on hype alone, or a cool Facebook ad featuring Floyd Mayweather, The Game or Paris Hilton (yes, there is one).

In the research phase of this book I looked at over 50 different small market cap cryptocurrencies, read the white papers, checked out the development teams and investigated if they had real world usage potential. From this initial group I narrowed down the final selection to 12 coins. These are my personal "best of the rest" in the cryptocurrency market, and the ones with most growth potential in 2018.

The price of these coins is not the singular reason you should invest in them. The market capitalization figure is far more important. For example, Ripple (XRP) tokens are priced around $0.18 but has a market cap of around $6 billion, making it a far more mature and structured asset, with less potential for large gains in the future.

In terms of general investing advice, diversification is important. However, if you have been in the cryptocurrency market for any length of time, you will know just how quickly things can move. This is even more so the case with these small market cap coins. My personal recommendation (just my recommendation - this is not financial advice) is that you have no more than **30%** of your total cryptocurrency portfolio in small cap coins like this. The rest should be placed in more stable investments such as Bitcoin and Ethereum.

One final note, this book is written with the assumption that you have some basic knowledge of cryptocurrency and the ideas surrounding it. If you're a complete cryptocurrency novice, I recommend one of my other books *Cryptocurrency: Beginners Bible* as it explains even the most elementary of cryptocurrency concepts.

Thanks,

Stephen

Factors to Consider Before Investing

While larger cryptocurrencies like Bitcoin, Ethereum and Litecoin have long track records and multiple real world functions, some of the coins mentioned in this book do not - hence their lower price.

There are a number of different variables to investigate before you undertake any investment, and cryptocurrency has its own set.

Proof of Concept (PoC)

In other words, does the technology have a working model, or is it still in a theoretical stage. Obviously more mature coins will have a higher value, with the more theoretical coins being a bigger risk. As the different coins here are in different stages of their life cycle, that is up for you to decide.

The development team

Who are the developers and what is their track record. Particularly within the cryptocurrency and blockchain space? Another thing to consider is their record within the particular industry they are targeting.

The utility of the coin

Ideas are great, but if the coin token itself doesn't have usage, then the true potential of the project must be questioned. This is especially true in the case of certain coins where the theory and market potential checks out, but the question of "why can I just use Bitcoin/Litecoin to do the same thing" is often raised.

The roadmap

Roadmaps are important for short-term gains because they set out development targets for the coin. If these goals are reached and the products/platforms move from alpha to beta to a fully launched product, then that only means positive things for the coin and its value.

Which exchanges the coin is listed on

Many of these coins are still only available on smaller exchanges. Once the coin is listed on larger exchanges (for example Bittrex), the coin has greater visibility and this leads to a rise in value.

Mining Algorithm - Proof of Work vs. Proof of Stake

You'll notice later on when discussing individual coins that I talk about which mining algorithms are used. The two most popular are Proof of Work (PoW), used by Bitcoin and Proof of Stake (PoS), which will be used by Ethereum from Q4 2017 and beyond, and is currently used by a number of Ethereum based tokens.

In my previous book *Bitcoin: Beginners Bible* I discussed why I don't recommend mining as an effective method for obtaining cryptocurrency, for the regular user. That still holds true for the majority of the coins listed in this book, but it's important to understand why the difference in mining algorithm matters.

Why do we need mining?

We need mining to ensure a transaction (or block) is correctly validated, in other words, we need to ensure the same transaction doesn't occur twice - known as the double spending problem. As a reward for validating this transaction, miners are rewarded with a tiny percentage of it (known as the network fee).

To put it bluntly, Proof of Work takes a lot more energy than Proof of Stake. A 2015 study showed that one Bitcoin transaction takes the equivalent daily energy of 1.57 US homes. Proof of Stake is also a fairer, more energy efficient system, which is a huge advantage for community based coins.

Minimizing Your Risk with Dollar Cost Averaging

One of the best ways to minimize your risk in a volatile market is to use what is known as 'dollar cost averaging'. This simply means dividing up your total planned investment and buying cryptocurrencies at regular intervals instead of all at once.

With dollar cost averaging, you are simply buying less of an asset (for this example, I will use Bitcoin) when the price is high, and more when the price is low. Your total exposure is less because you are only exposed to part of any decline in the market, as opposed to all of it with a lump sum investment. Your average cost per coin is therefore likely to be lower.

Let's use an example, both Jamal and Rachel have $1200 to invest in Bitcoin at the start of 2015. Jamal decides to invest all $1200 on January 1st, Rachel on the other hand is going to use dollar cost averaging. She will invest $100 on the 1st of each month, for a total of $1200. The prices used in this example are the actual Bitcoin trading prices as of those dates.

January 1st 2015 - $305.32

February 1st 2015 - $237.18

March 1st 2015 - $263.57

April 1st 2015 - $255.23

May 1st 2015 - $226.45

June 1st 2015 - $233.44

July 1st 2015 - $260.73

August 1st 2015 -$283.04

September 1st 2015 - $229.00

October 1st 2015 - $240.10

November 1st 2015 - $325.28

December 1st 2015 - $375.95

Jamal's total investment in BTC = 3.93 (1200/305.32)

Rachel's total investment in BTC = 4.55 (1200/269.60)

Price on January 1st 2016 - $433.57

Jamal's Portfolio Value = 3.93*433.57 = $1704.02

Rachel's Portfolio Value = 4.55*433.57 = $1974.37

Jamal's ROI = 42%

Rachel's ROI = 64.5%

So by using dollar cost averaging, Rachel's average BTC purchase price was $269.60, whereas Jamal bought a lump sum at $305.32. By having a lower average purchase price, Rachel's ROI is higher over time. Jamal bought his coins at the peak of the market before a prolonged downturn, whereas Rachel utilized this downturn to her advantage.

Remember, time in the market beats timing the market. Generally speaking, the longer you are invested in something, the better.

Why you shouldn't touch a coin in the initial Post-ICO period

I made a conscious decision not to include any cryptocurrencies that were within 1 month of the end of their ICO. For those who are unware, an ICO is an initial coin offering, and a common method for companies behind cryptocurrencies to gain investment. Like IPOs in the stock world, a total portion of the company is sold to the public. Investors donate Bitcoin or Ethereum, and in return they are given a number of cryptocurrency tokens from the ICO. For example, in the case of Neblio, those donating were rewarded with 20,000 NEBL for every 1 Bitcoin donated. Though it should be noted that unlike IPOs, with an ICO, you do not own a % of the company, merely the tokens associated with it.

The post ICO period is extremely volatile price wise, and not a good period for anyone to enter the market, especially if you are an inexperienced cryptocurrency investor.

The reason for this volatility is often linked to ICOs offering a pre-sale bonus for early investors, who then sell their bonus in the post-ICO period for a quick profit, which ends up causing the price to fall. Usually, once the month after the ICO has ended, the price tends to become more stable.

All of the coins discussed in this book have been out of the ICO period for at least 1 month (many for years). Investing during the ICO period is a different matter, if you choose to do so for future coins, I advise you to read any instructions carefully so you don't send any coins to the incorrect wallet address.

7 Giant Mistakes Guaranteed to Cost You Money

1. Not double checking all links (including the ones in this book)

Unfortunately, phishing scams are rife in the cryptocurrency space. Just this week, I saw 3 new ones either via email, paid search traffic (Google ads) or from reading about them on cryptocurrency message boards. Remember to check any link you click that is asking for you username, password or any other personal details.

2. Storing your cryptocurrency on an exchange

While rare, exchange attacks do happen, and cryptocurrency does get stolen. If you move your cryptocurrency off an exchange and into a private wallet, hackers cannot touch it (provided that wallet follows proper security measures). For each of the coins mentioned, I have included the appropriate wallet information for them.

3. Giving your private key to anyone

Your private key is what you need to send cryptocurrency from your wallet. You should never give this to anyone, for any reason. Keep it secure, preferably written on a piece of paper that is stored inside a physical safe. Never keep your private key on a server, and never enter it on a public Wi-Fi network.

4. Panic selling during a dip in the market

Unless you need the money to feed your family, there is ZERO reason to sell your cryptocurrency at a loss during a dip in the market. Remember, this investment should represent a small percentage of your overall investing portfolio, in other words - you can afford to take a small loss on paper. More often than not in the cryptocurrency market, waiting it out, and long term holding, is the best investment strategy.

5. Not using dollar cost averaging when buying

Time in the market beats timing the market. You can minimize your risk by using dollar cost averaging and spreading your investment out over time. This prevents getting burned by buying at the top of the market.

6. Not doing your research/due diligence

This book is designed to be a comprehensive introduction to these cryptocurrencies, but it is certainly not the only resource available. I encourage you to do your own research in addition to what I've provided in this book. The best source for information will come from the coin's own website and white paper (although at times white papers can read more like a press release than a technical document, this alone is a good indicator).

7. Borrowing money to invest in cryptocurrencies

This really should be obvious, but I've personally witnessed it too many times that I feel it needs to be reiterated. You should NEVER borrow money to invest in anything, let alone a market as volatile as cryptocurrency. Losing your own money is one thing, losing someone else's money is another. So, next time you're considering borrowing money from a bank, or using your student loan to invest - don't. Trust me, it's not worth it.

Bonus tip/mistake 7.5 - Checking the price of your investment on a daily basis

Just leave it alone - trust me

How to Buy Bitcoin

Gone are the days when buying Bitcoin was a time consuming and somewhat uncomfortable endeavor. Nowadays buying Bitcoin is a similar process to exchanging currency when you go on vacation.

There are two ways to buy Bitcoin, the first is to use fiat currency (USD, EUR, GBP etc.) to purchase cryptocurrency via an exchange. These exchanges function the same way as regular foreign currency exchanges do. The prices fluctuate on a daily basis, and like regular currency exchange markets - they are open 24/7. These exchanges make their money from charging a small fee for each transaction.

Some charge both buyers and sellers, some only charge a fee for buying. For security reasons, most of these exchanges will require you to verify your ID before allowing you to purchase cryptocurrency.

It is also important to note the type of payments each exchange supports. Some allow for debit/credit card payments whereas other only accept PayPal or bank wire transfers. Below are the three biggest and reputable currency exchanges for purchasing Bitcoin, Ethereum and other altcoins with fiat currency like US dollars, Euros or British Pounds.

Coinbase

Currently largest currency exchange in the world, Coinbase allows users to buy, sell and store cryptocurrency. Coinbase is undoubtedly the most beginner friendly exchange for anyone looking to get involved in the cryptocurrency market. They currently allow trading of Bitcoin, as well as, Ethereum and LiteCoin using fiat currency as a base. Known for their stellar security procedures and insurance policies regarding stored currency. The exchange also has a fully functioning iPhone and Android app for buying and selling on the go, very useful if you are looking to trade.

Once you are signed up and complete the identity verification procedures you can buy Bitcoin with your credit or debit card instantly.

Coinbase also recently launched the Coinbase Vault, which is a secure way of storing your cryptocurrency while still having it accessible to trade. The vault uses double email address + phone verification in order to access your funds. If you're planning on holding long-term, I still recommend offline storage - but as an intermediary option, the Vault is a step in the right direction.

If you sign up for Coinbase using this link, you will receive $10 worth of free Bitcoin after your first purchase of more than $100 worth of cryptocurrency.

http://bit.ly/10dollarbtc

Note, if you're going to be trading Bitcoin, I recommend doing so on Coinbase's partner platform GDax, which has lower fees.

Bittrex

Based and regulated in the USA, Bittrex is a great exchange to buy altcoins for Bitcoin or Ethereum. With over 190 different cryptocurrencies, it is the most comprehensive in terms of altcoin support.

Their support isn't as good as Coinbase's, and you'll have to transfer the coins to a wallet if you want to securely store them long-term, but for trading altcoins - you can't go wrong with Bittrex.

Poloniex

With more than 100 different cryptocurrencies available and data analysis for advanced traders, Poloniex is the most comprehensive exchange on the market. Low trading fees are another plus, this is a great place to trade your Bitcoin into other cryptocurrencies. If you have never purchased Bitcoin before, you will no be able to do so as Poloniex does not allow fiat currency deposits. Therefore, you will have to make your initial Bitcoin purchases on Coinbase or Kraken.

Buying Locally

The second way to buy Bitcoins in exchange for fiat currency is to locally purchase them in person. The advantage of this is that you may be able to get a marginally better price than by using an exchange. The other advantage is that users living in countries that don't have easy access to online exchanges can still buy coins in person. All transactions are protected by Escrow to prevent either party being scammed.

Website http://localbitcoins.com is the current market leader for local bitcoin transactions with sellers in over 15,000 cities around the world.

Transferring your newly purchased Bitcoin to your exchange of choice.

Once you have bought your Bitcoin from Coinbase/Kraken, you'll need to then transfer it over the Binance, Bittrex or whichever exchange your coin of choice is listed on. To do this, simply go to the exchange you need to transfer the coins to (e.g. Bittrex) and click on "deposit", choose BTC (remember to double check you've clicked the correct coin). This will generate an address that looks like this 1F1tAaz5x1HUXrCNLbtMDqcw6o5GNn4xqX

From there, go to your Coinbase/Kraken BTC wallet and select "send", then in the "recipient" section copy the BTC address of the new exchange. Double check the amount of BTC you are sending, then click send and the transfer will initiate. Most of the time transfers take around 10 minutes, however some exchanges take longer to process. Once your transfer is complete you can then exchange your BTC for any of the altcoins listed below.

Storing Your Coins - How to set up MyEtherWallet

Many of these coins are based on the Ethereum blockchain, and therefore use ERC20 tokens. Therefore, these tokens can be stored in Ethereum wallets. Wallets can be daunting to set up at first, so I recommend you use something simple to get started, the most convenient of these is MyEtherWallet.

Step-by-Step guide to setting up MyEtherWallet

1. Go to https://www.myetherwallet.com/

2. Enter a strong but easy to remember password. Do not forget it.

3. This encrypts (protects) your private key. It does not generate your private key. This password alone will not be enough to access your coins.

4. Click the "Generate Wallet" button.

5. Download your Keystore/UTC file & save this file to a USB drive.

6. This is the encrypted version of your private key. You need your password to access it. It is safer than your unencrypted private key but you must have your password to access it in the future.

7. Read the warning. If you understand it, click the "I understand. Continue" button.

8. Print your paper wallet backup and/or carefully hand-write the private key on a piece of paper.

9. If you are writing it, I recommend you write it 2 or 3 times. This decreases the chance your messy handwriting will prevent you from accessing your wallet later.

10. Copy & paste your address into a text document somewhere.

11. Search your address on https://etherscan.io/ Bookmark this page as this is how you can view your balance at any time

12. Send a small amount of any coin from your previous wallet or exchange to your new wallet - just to ensure you have everything correct

Hardware Wallets

Another safe, offline solution is to use a hardware wallet. The most popular of these being Trezor and Nano S. Both of these cost around $100, but represent a convenient, yet safe way to store your cryptocurrency. Further explanation of hardware wallets is in my first book *Cryptocurrency: Beginners Bible*.

12 Exclusive Coins Under $1 with Potential for Huge Profits

District0x (DNT)

Price at Time of Writing - $0.039

Market Cap at Time of Writing - $23,255,100

Available on:

BTC: Binance, Bittrex, Liqui

Where to store:

District0x is currently an ERC20 token and can be stored on My Ether Wallet. You can view how to add DNT as a custom token on https://etherscan.io/token/district0x

District0x has the goal of breaking the internet down into smaller, more manageable pieces. If you've ever seen the movie The Hunger Games, you'll remember each district was focused on a single task: District 7 was the lumber district, District 8 focused on textile production, District 9 with grain etc.

District0x plans to do the same thing with the blockchain technology and Decentralized Autonomous Organizations (DAO). Each district will have its own payment and invoicing system, along with complete self governance. The venture will use the Ethereum blockchain to run smart contracts.

What District0x has done to make to the process user friendly, is combine different necessary (like smart contracts and payment processing) elements into a package, so it's not essential for users to completely understand the technology behind the platform. You can think of this as similar to how Wordpress works for web development. At the core of every district is the ability to operate a market or a bulletin board application.

Currently, there are over 100 district ideas in play. Theoretically, it would allow an individual such as you or me to implement their own version of AirBNB, Craigslist or Uber, without having to go through a middleman like the current system has to. This in turn reduces transaction fees and makes the overall cost lower for all parties involved. There are no fees to create districts, which makes them available to everyone. Currently, refundable deposits are required to put forward a district proposal, once the district passes quality control checks (ensuring the district is not there for malicious intent), the deposit is refunded to the district creator.

One such idea already running is Ethlance, an online freelancing platform similar to Upwork or Fiverr, but without the large transaction fees. Interestingly enough, the District0x team has actually hired developers via Ethlance to help them execute the project.

Another promising proposal is ShipIt, which focuses on the multi-billion dollar shipping industry. The idea is to create a decentralized maritime logistics platform. The sheer number of transactions in this industry alone (trucking, forwarding, warehousing etc.) make this a perfect foil for a blockchain solution.

The framework is in place, however the team needs to do more to gather traction, plus a larger user base to utilize their own districts. The current team is small, with just 10 members, plus an additional advisor, but there will certainly be additions in the future as the project continues to grow. Progress reports are frequent and developments are regular posted on GitHub.

One interesting approach the District0x team are employing is creating a free "education portal" to inform the wider public about the platform, and the real world functionality of districts. They are doing this are they believe the current limiting factor is a general ignorance of the potential of the platform. The portal is scheduled for rollout in Q4 2017.

District0x tokens (DNT) can be used to fund project and stake voting rights in different districts, the more tokens one has, the greater of a say they have. The one issue here is a possible abuse of a "pay to play" system.

The decentralized element of District0x means there is no single point of failure, for example there is no single server that all of the individual districts run from. This ensures that targeted hacking attacks cannot take down the entire network.

Supply wise, there are 600 million DNT available, with a total projected supply of 1 billion. It should be noted that in the white paper, the District0x team does reserve the right to add additional coins to the total supply, however this is contingent on the exchange rate between ETH/USD. For example, if ETH's value declines significantly vs. USD, the team can add additional coins to account for this fluctuation. This isn't necessarily something to be concerned about (financial hedging occurs all the time in fiat markets), but it's definitely something worth nothing.

Listing on larger exchanges will help spike the price in the short term. The team are in ongoing discussions with large exchange Bittrex, and a listing on there could easily see price rises of 100%. Long term prices will be largely determined by the number of popular districts that are set up using the platform. The next two planned district launches are Name Bazaar and Meme Factory.

Neblio (NEBL)

Price at Time of Writing - $0.984

Market Cap at Time of Writing - $12,220,794

Available on:

BTC: Cryptopia

Where to store?

Wallets can be downloaded from https://nebl.io/wallets/

Based out of the USA, Neblio aims to provide a simple blockchain solution to the business sector. The project was born out of a need to simplify currently complex blockchain tools in order to achieve wider adoption within the business sector.

Taking into account blockchain solutions for transparent data, plus reliability and security owing to a lack of central server - the technology has a huge advantage for businesses over traditional methods. However, cost of maintenance, and difficulty of integration have made uptake in the business world somewhat slower than blockchain enthusiasts would like. Certain industries are waiting for more mature blockchain solutions to appear, rather than take a risk on technology that is unproven in their particularly sector. The Neblio team plan to streamline this process and make blockchain solutions more accessible for businesses as a whole.

A real world example of this would be a doctor's office needing to access patient records. Rather than use a traditional central database, that is liable to server downtime, or cyber attacks - they could use a blockchain solution which provides the same data, but without the risks. This same system could be used for any business that needs to utilize frequent audits, as the data would be unalterable with a record of who altered it and when.

Neblio plans to support current popular programming languages give it a great advantage in this area. Developers in languages such as Python, Java, Javascript and PHP won't be forced to learn a new programming language to develop applications on the Neblio blockchain. This is an area that is vital if the platform wants to attract developers to Neblio versus other platforms. This also makes Neblio applications compatible with mobile devices running iOS or Android.

In terms of competitor coins, the space is extremely competitive with giants such as Ethereum and Neo already occupying some of the real estate. Stratis is another big one, however, Stratis has had a year headstart and in terms of development, yet Neblio is already neck-and-neck in terms of having a working product.

The beta version of the Neblio network is currently scheduled for a launch in Q3 2018, with a larger scale marketing campaign due in Q2 of the same year. The team has been extremely active in developments, and recently both an iOS and Android wallet were both launched ahead of schedule.

Supply wise, there are approximately 12.5 million NEBL tokens in circulation currently, with a total supply of 13 million. NEBL tokens can be used as a means of exchange on the Neblio network

There is certainly a gap in the market for this type of blockchain solution. However, Neblio's future may lie with working within a specific industry, as the goal of solely providing broad "enterprise solution" is one that is susceptible to a large amount of competition, particularly from vast entities like Ethereum and Neo.

Bytom (BTM)

Price at Time of Writing - $0.069

Market Cap at Time of Writing - $80,324,168

Available on:

Fiat: Cryptopia (NZ)

BTC: Cryptopia, BTER (CN), Bit9 (CN)

Where to store?:

Bytom is currently an ERC20 token and can be stored on My Ether Wallet. You can view how to add Bytom as a custom token on Ethplorer via http://bit.ly/bytomwallet

Bytom is a true sleeper coin. Coming out of China, it's only natural that the coin has received initial comparisons to NEO (formerly Antshares), one of the most talked about cryptocurrencies of 2017.

Although their official Whitepaper is currently only available in Chinese, the roughly translated opening reads as "Bytom will not be another Bitcoin, or an Ethereum 2.0. Bytom is an intermediary connecting generalized blockchains with specialized blockchains." The whitepaper then goes on to discuss the idea of connecting physical and digital assets while resolving issues like compliance and trustworthiness.

In laymen's terms, Bytom has the potential for offline assets to be registered on the blockchain. In their own words, "bridging the online world and the atomic world". This bridging allows users to seamlessly swap between digital assets (like cryptocurrencies), and physical ones. This is something that no other cryptocurrency in development promises to utilize.

Real world applications for the technology include the management of income assets and dividend distribution for investors.

A very strong development team is headed up by Chiang Jia, who previously founded 8BTC - one of China's largest resources for cryptocurrency news and insights. Anyone who has been involved in the cryptocurrency market will understand just how important news from China is in affecting the price of Bitcoin and other crypto assets. The CEO was invited to speak at the 2017 Global Blockchain Summit.

Another determinant of the price is the viability of mining. Bytom has embraced the popular AI ASIC friendly mining algorithm. China is currently the world's largest base for cryptocurrency mining, with 70% of the entire mining work done in the Middle Kingdom. Part of Bytom's plan is to reward miners at a technological level as well as a financial one. CEO Jia stated in a June interview with 8BTC that "As for the mining industry, the outdated mining farm could be transformed into data center that provides AI hardware acceleration service." Chinese miners tend to support their own currencies, which is part of the reason for NEO's success in 2017. If Bytom can replicate this at even a fraction of the uptake, it will only mean good things going forward.

One particular thing to note about Bytom, is the team's dedication to continued, if somewhat slow progress. However, you can look at this in a positive light. Rather than succumbing to spending their entire budget on marketing like other coins, Bytom's roadmap is well laid out with realistic goals. You don't need to expect life changing developments within the next 6 months for example. But a solid alpha product in Q1 2018 could certainly lead to decent short term gains. Right now, the scheduled release of v1.0 of the Bytom blockchain is due in Q2 2018.

Other notable figures include Long Yu, a former Senior System Engineer at Alipay, a huge Chinese POS payment system (similar to Apple Pay or Samsung Pay).

In early September the Bytom team took home 2nd prize in a field of over 100 competitors in the 2017 Cosmos Hackathon, a blockchain network designed to solve problems like scalability and interoperability. 2nd Place is currently the best achievement from a Chinese team at the competition.

The roadmap shows that by early 2018, many of Bytom's most exciting features will be put to market, in beta form. A large press conference for the release of their alpha product is scheduled for Q1 2018.

Currently Bytom is in a unique place where there are no strict competitor coins.

The have been some blips in the development stages already, with Bytom removing the coin from Binance in mid August. However the coin is now listed on Cryptopia, which while being a small exchange compared to giants like Bittrex and Poloniex, does make it accessible to the US and western market. The Chinese market has easy access with direct BTN/CNY trades available on the BTC9 exchange. Those holding ETH can exchange it for Bytom at the BTER exchange.

Bytom's value comes from the fee each user will have to pay to use the Bytom blockchain. Holding Bytom coins essentially represents shares in the blockchain itself. Bytom believes strongly in this community based ownership model, and their concept of "distributed autonomy" is one that they hold dearly to the project. The aim is structure the management system for a balance between efficiency and fairness.

Circulating supply is high at 664 million BTN currently available, with a projected total supply of 2.1 billion BTN. Of this total supply, 7% is reserved for private equity groups and angel investors, whose funds will be used in the technology's initial development stages.

Overall, Bytom might not make any major price movements in the next 2 months, but as soon as 2018 rolls around, the coin has potential to make a big impact in the blockchain space.

Note: On some cryptocurrency exchanges, Bitmark will be listed as BTM, these two currencies are not related. Double check before executing a trade.

Golem (GNT)

Price at time of writing - $0.267

Market Cap at time of writing - $222,516,176

Available on:

Fiat: Yunbi (CN)

BTC: Poloniex, Bittrex, Liqui

Where to store?

Golem is an ERC20 token so can be stored in MyEtherWallet

Golen is a coin token, based on Ethereum blockchain technology. With nearly 10 months since the original ICO, Golem is somewhat of a granddad in the cryptocurrency world. Described by some commentators as the "AirBNB of computing", the value of the coin is centered around the tasks that can be accomplished using it.

The founders of the Golem Project refer to it as a "supercomputer", with the ability to interconnect with other computers for various purposes. These include scientific research, data analysis and cryptocurrency mining. For example, if your computer has unused, or idle power, using the Golem network, you can rent that power (hence the AirBNB comparison) to someone else who needs it. The user who needs the extra power, has the ability to access supercomputer levels of processing power for a fraction of the cost of actually owning the processing power themselves. Like other Ethereum based projects, the decentralized element provides an additional layer of security as there is no single point of failure on the network. The first use case of the network's alpha release was using shared processing power to produce a 3D CGI rendering.

One fantastic potential usage for this power is the ability for a company to prevent downtime during a urge of users. There are many examples of websites being down during periods of unusually high demand, such as waiting for a livestream of a popular event to start. One notable example of this is Rockstar's website crashing during the release of the Grand Theft Auto 4 trailer. Using idle power from other computers on the Golem network, has the potential to prevent issues like this from occurring in the future.

The growth of such services is currently in demand in the non-crypto space, with cloud computing services accounting for roughly $175 billion global turnover in 2015. For example, Amazon's Amazon Web Services (AWS) business is an increasing part of the online giant's overall holdings.

If you look at Golem vs. Traditional cryptocurrency mining, Golem is definitely a step ahead. Because it only utilizes idle power, there is no wasted energy, which traditional mining suffers from a lot of. Even for a casual user, the ability to offset some of their electricity costs is a big positive.

The ability for users to earn money for their unused computing power is, in theory, a no-brainer, however what remains to be seen is the practical application of the technology. The Golem team's lack of marketing visibility also appears to hurt the coins value in recent times. The lack of ability to buy GNT using fiat currency (such as USD) is also a drawback for the mass market, however for small cap coins, that is somewhat of a given at this stage of the overall cryptocurrency lifecycle.

Supply wise, 1 billion GNT tokens were generated during the ICO, and that is the sum total that will be available for the lifetime of the project. Tokens will be used as a transfer of value on the Golem network.

It should be noted that the technology is still very much in the early development stages and as of August 2017, the team are still looking for alpha testers for the project. The Golem Project has a very real possibility of petering out into nothing. On the flip side - there is tremendous potential for large future gains with the price of a coin still under $0.30.

Tron (TRX)

Price at time of writing - $0.0018

Market Cap at time of writing - $125,420,800

Available on:

BTC: Liqui

ETH: Liqui, EtherDelta

Even in small and medium cap cryptocurrencies, Tron is a true wildcard. Lead by Justin Sun, known in China as "The next Jack Ma", and part of Forbes Asia 30 Under 30 - the project is one with wide reaching implications for the in-app currency movement.

You can think of Tron as both a facilitator for in-game or in-app transactions (also known as microtransactions) and as a way of increasing the value of your own content.

The biggest trend in video games for the past 5 years has been the rise in in-game microtransactions, also known as the pay-to-win model. This frustrates gamers as any assets they have built up in game 1, are not transferable to game 2. For example, take the popular mobile game Clash of Clans. The game features a huge amount of microtransactions, and players have spent hundreds of dollars building up their in-game assets. Currently there are only very limited ways for him to sell those assets in exchange for money. Plus, if a new game comes out and the gamer wants to try it out, they'd have to start from the bottom and work their way up again. Tron would allow said gamer to transfer his Clash of Clans assets over to the new game in exchange for a small transaction fee.

Content creators can also use Tron as a payment system for their content. Similar to how YouTube users use Patreon donations as a method of making additional income from their content.

The development team continues to grow, and the recent announcement of one of Alibaba's (the Amazon of China) chief engineers joining the project is another coup for the Tron team.

The future of Tron will depends of two things. The first is adoption, which games will support TRX as a middleman for cross-game transactions? Secondly would these games choose TRX over the coins currently available like BTC or LTC. Like many of the coins mentioned in the book, they idea in theory is a multi-billion dollar one, but does the token have enough utility to warrant it?

Supply wise, Tron is huge. With over 40 billion TRX coins currently in circulation, with a projected total of 100 billion. However, as the coin is designed to facilitate microtransactions (fractions of a cent), a large supply is needed.

In a show of good faith, in early October 2017, the Tron team air dropped 500 TRX coins into the wallet of everyone with an account on the exchange liqui.io. Air drops like this have useful community building and general awareness effects.

Aeon (AEON)

Price at time of writing - $0.84

Market Cap at time of writing - $12,359,745

Available on:

BTC: Bittrex

If you've read my first book *Cryptocurrency: Beginners Bible*, you'll remember I talked about Monero (the price has risen 3x since the release of said book) being the only truly private cryptocurrency currently on the planet. Well, that's no longer the case. You can think of Aeon as Monero's little brother. In a market of overhyped, overbought ICOs and heavily marketed copycat projects, Aeon brings lightweight innovation - the coin is a mobile-friendly, decentralized digital currency.

The team behind Aeon feature some of the core Monero developers - in the words of Aeon's founders "everybody's main internet device continues to be their cellphone, a device with a low-powered CPU and limited available storage. Aeon is about enabling this era, enabling an age where all people everywhere have the freedom to privately send and receive money with whatever gadget they already own."

By focusing on smaller transactions like this, Aeon aims to take a firm hold on the daily consumer market, all while offering a completely private service. So why the need for privacy? Frankly, many of us are sick and tired of our data being stored on central servers, privy to anyone that wants to take a look. Aeon uses cryptography to completely encrypt the information of both the sender and receiver in a transaction. Therefore, the identifying information of each user is not available on the blockchain itself. This is compounded with what is known as "ring signatures", which means the funds are untraceable.

Aeon will often be compared to Monero, however the faster blockchain verifications (thanks to their lighter weight Proof of Work algorithm) allow transaction to process faster, making it more useful for day-to-day use. You could look at the relationship similar to Litecoin's relationship with Bitcoin.

The lightweight features of Aeon allow users to run a full node on their mobile, this speeds up transactions due to no longer needing a third party app running a public node. Another addition area where Aeon shines is by using a limited amount of storage space on a given device, this reduces the likelihood of any age-based attacks on your mobile or laptop.

One area that could be seen as a drawback for Aeon is the lack of a publicly released roadmap. This is due to an extremely small development team, of officially just 1 person at the time of writing. However, Aeon's open source code is publicly available, and everyone is welcome to contribute to the project, in a similar vein to Monero - which benefited greatly from a enthusiastic community. A community generated development fund currently stands at over $400,000 - which is far higher than other coins with much larger market caps. This fund will be used to attract elite developers to the project in the short and medium term.

Supply wise, Aeon has a relatively small number of coins released at around 14.5 million. For those into mining, Aeon currently offers some of the better rewards in the cryptocurrency mining space, plus in theory their lightweight nodes could allow for efficient mobile mining (albeit for significantly reduced rewards).

Where Aeon's future growth may lie is a release their mobile wallet in the short term and wider adoption of private cryptocurrencies in the long term. This is one coin that certainly has gamechanging potential.

RISE (RISE)

Price at Time of Writing - $0.401

Market Cap at Time of Writing - $45,404,571

Available on:

Fiat: Litebit.eu (EUR)

BTC: Bittrex, YoBit

Where to store?

You can download RISE wallets for desktop (Windows, Mac and Linux) from the Rise website
http://rise.vision

RISE is an ecosystem for developers, businesses, tech startups, investors and device users. The platform offers decentralized applications and the creation of smart contracts. The platform aims to increase adoption of RISE versus competitor platforms by providing Software Development Kits (SDKs), so that RISE applications can be run on Windows, Mac and Linux. The platform also supports popular programming languages like Javascript, Python and Ruby. There's also a RISE investment platform where RISE holders can pool resources together to invest in projects.

Where RISE really shines is their "blockchain incubator" service for startup Decentralized Apps (DApps). These developers can use the RISE platform to develop their companies/coins, and RISE holders will be entitled to 20% of these coins when the product successfully launches. While RISE isn't the first cryptocurrency to offer a form of passive income like this, a 20% reward is far higher than competing coins.

The two current projects built using the RISE platform are Interlet and Chipz. Interlet is an Ethereum based person-to-person vacation platform that aims to compete with AirBNB, by charging a much lower fee to operate. Anyone who has used AirBNB in the past will know about often ridiculous fees (up to 20% of the vacation price) that AirBNB takes as a middleman, and Interlet plans to use this is a basis for providing competition.

The second project is Chipz, an online casino platform due for launch in Q1 2018. Those who hold RISE will be given a % of Chipz tokens based on how much RISE they hold at the time of launch. Chipz plans to integrate with the Waves platform so that holders of the token can directly exchange their Chipz for fiat currency, which in theory will make the casino a lot more accessible. A successful launch of Chipz will certainly mean good things for the price of RISE in the short term.

Competition wise, RISE can be compared to Ark and Lisk in broad terms. However, RISE offers token holders a much bigger share of DApp coins launched on the platform at 20% when compared to Ark's 5%.

The roadmap is an area where RISE is lacking when compared to other coins mentioned in this book. Projects are in the pipeline, including the release of Interlet, as well as a mobile friendly version of RISE. However, a lack of dates for these releases is something that the RISE team needs to address to inspire investor confidence.

That being said, the RISE team is a strong one, with 10 developers, many of which have a long and successful history in the blockchain and cryptocurrency space. One area I particularly like is the weekly release of a RISE newsletter, these 4 page posts give updates on the RISE ecosystem, as well as announcing team members, and any new projects in development. Easily digestible new bites like this are useful if you don't come from a tech or development background, or are more interested in the business side of things.

The RISE community continues to grow rapidly, and often times community driven initiatives can help maintain and increase the coin's value over time.

Supply wise, RISE currently has 114 million tokens in circulation. The utility of these tokens has already been discussed, and there are strong use cases both as voting tools and as a currency to be traded. The trading volume is very high for a coin of RISE's size, and this bodes well for it as an investment tool as it is less susceptible to price manipulation than coins with lower trading volumes.

Funfair (FUN)

Price at Time of Writing - $0.026

Market Cap at Time of Writing - $100,375,472

Where to store?

FUN tokens are ERC 20 tokens, so you can add them to MyEtherWallet by using the following information:

Address: 0xbbb1bd2d741f05e144e6c4517676a15554fd4b8d

Token symbol: FUN

Decimal places: 8

Funfair is a decentralized gaming platform powered by Ethereum smart contracts, based out of London and Singapore. Powering the creation of "smart casinos", the platform is attempting to capitalize on the potential $40 billion a year online gambling industry, an industry which has increased by 50% since 2010 and in projected to increase by another 50% by 2020.

The platform's main aims are to facilitate the building of online casinos with 3D games that can be built with current technology (namely HTML5) for both desktop and mobile platforms. In terms of gas costs (Ethereum transactions fees), these will be up to 10x cheaper than current online casino platforms.

As the games are executed with the use of Ethereum smart contracts, their fairness is not in question. The random number generated is transparent on the blockchain so anyone can see the results are truly randomized, and not artificially in favor of the house. This ensures that no one is being cheated by the casino operator.

Cryptocurrency gaming in itself is not a new phenomenon, in fact Bitcoin casinos have been running for years. However, the fluctuations in the currency itself, along with notoriously slow payouts and lack of regulation, has yet to see mainstream adoption.

The development team is built largely of members with previous experience in game creation. Founder and Angel Investor Jez San has a storied history in the gaming sector and helped play a part in the creation of multi-million dollar selling video games like Star Fox, while recently his experience lies in the online gaming space at leading online poker website PKR.com, before leaving the site to focus on Funfair. These connections could play a vital role in the adoption of Funfair within the gaming space, which is undoubtedly the number one challenge it faces going forward.

There are already complete 3D games built using the platform, which means the technology is now firmly beyond the theoretical stage, and into the execution stage. The Funfair launch suite itself already has 6 games under construction, which will be used as playable prototypes at industry events.

It is important to note that Funfair's value will not just come from the operation of 1 casino. Licensing the software itself will potentially create thousands of online casinos, which in turn will be in significantly more revenue than a centralized model. However, the challenge of getting that initial casino to decide to use the platform is a large one.

The main problem that has previously plagued this sector the transaction fees that occur with every new game or spin. This has led to other blockchain casinos suffering from slow playing times and costly fees to play. After all, nobody wants to have to wait 30 seconds between blackjack hands or between dice rolls for roulette. There's also a limit with the number of players that can play at one time. Current technology has a general rule of about 10 players per table, whereas with blockchain technology, the number, in theory, is unlimited.

The transactions costs are estimated to be at a ridiculous $1 per hand for blockchain based blackjack games and $0.75 per bet on dice games. With typical bet sizes, this represents around 10% per hand. Transactions costs have a further effect, because of the house edge of casino games. Even with higher bets minimizing the cost per hand, the house edge + transaction costs are simply too large for the player to even have a chance of profiting in the long term. Funfair's aim to reduce these will lead to a much higher uptake from players. One of Funfair's key goals is to reduce player transaction costs to a much more manageable 0.1% per hand.

Supply wise, over 3 billion FUN tokens were generated in the ICO - with no further token due to be generated during Funfair's life cycle . The sounds like a large number, however it is important to note that many of this are designed to be "burned" as transaction fees for the games themselves.The FUN token value itself will be utilized in a number of ways. Including for playing the games themselves, paying affiliates (which is a significant part of the online casino industry), and paying the game creators themselves.

Mothership (MSP)

Price at Time of Writing - $0.167

Market Cap at Time of Writing - $23,389,520

Where to store?
MSP token are ERC20 tokens so can be stored on MyEtherWallet

Mothership is one of the most intriguing cryptocurrencies on the market today. Built on the Ethereum platform, the coin's aim is to make cryptocurrency markets accessible for EU companies and Estonian e-Residents.

To truly understand Mothership, it's important to first understand Estonian e-residency, and how that process works.

E-residency takes place in the form of an Estonian government issued "digital ID card", which is combined with an authorized digital signature. The signature is legally binding and allows anyone in the world to register an EU company online. This gives unprecedented access to the European market. In a time where previously repressed parts of the world are looking for ways to attract new business and investment, Estonia is certainly at the forefront of this movement.

Where Mothership comes in, is that for blockchain businesses, it allows incorporation in Estonia, with 100% remote online access. A bank account will be provided, which is then linked with the built-in cryptocurrency exchange. Estonia also offers 0% corporation tax for companies inside the e-residency scheme. This is an extremely attractive proposition for blockchain companies that were previously forced to operate in countries with less friendly regulation, both in terms of the legality of cryptocurrency based firms, and general business tax laws.

The project entails three parts. A cryptocurrency exchange with 24/7 access to the markets, which combined with automatic identification (linked to your e-residency) makes the transactions from cryptocurrency to fiat currency near instant. Anyone who has signed up to a cryptocurrency exchange will know the pains of having to wait days (or even sometimes months) for identity verification.

The built-in cryptocurrency wallet is connected to your e-residency, which provides an automatic digital signature, which in turn protects your funds from fraudulent activity.

The e-residency program continues to grow, and Estonia estimates more than 10 million e-residents by 2025. Government support is one area that many crypto-based assets lack, whereas Mothership has been truly embraced by the Estonian government.

The project's timeline is publicly available to view on Trello. The short-term goals include launching the beta version of the MSP token market whereas the actual exchange itself is planned for a launch between Q1 and Q2 2018. This is also the time period where the team plans to launch the e-residence wallet.

Supply wise, there will are currently 140 million MSP tokens, with an additional 60 million planned in the future.

The inherent risk to the Mothership project is that they are not specifically offering anything *new* to the market. There are already hundreds of cryptocurrency exchanges. However, the tie-in with the e-residency scheme, and the instantaneous swapping between cryptocurrency and fiat makes the project an attractive one in the short-to-medium term at the very least.

OKCash (OK)

Price at Time of Writing - $0.317

Market Cap at Time of Writing - $23,143,613

Where to store?

You can download the official OKCash wallet (available for both desktop and Android) from https://okcash.org/

Available on:

Fiat: Litebit.eu (EUR)

BTC: Bittrex, Cryptopia

Dubbing itself "the future of cash", OKCash plans to operate a worldwide payment system for microtransactions. With no cross-border payments and near instant confirmation times, the platform plans to target those in countries where bank account usage is not widespread. In other words, people have the ability to make payments to one another without needing a bank account.

The low-fee system allows OKCash to be useful for small donations or even online tipping. These tips can be made public and donations can be made over social networks for greater visibility. This could even be used in the case of emergencies to transfer funds fast to those affected.

While other cryptocurrencies promise similar things with regard to microtransactions and quick payments, where OKCash shines is the extremely low payment fee. There is no fee to receive a payment and the current fee to send OK coins is just 0.0001 OK, or $0.00003

One cool feature of the OKCash wallet is a built-in encrypted messaging system to protect users privacy.

OKCash has seen some strong initial adoption, with over 136,000 OKCash wallets being created already, and more than 19,000 addresses holding at least 1000 OK coins.

The proof-of-stake mining algorithm ensures minimal wasted energy when compared to a traditional proof-of-work algorithm (used by Bitcoin). The decentralized model also allows anyone to contribute to the OKCash network.

The team's marketing efforts have been unique and quite successful so far. A focus on video games has led to OKCash being a prize in both Minecraft and FIFA tournaments so far, with more projects like this to come in the near future.

The development team, and their lack of public visibility is an area that OK is lacking in. Although their site lists more than 40 team members, all of them currently go by pseudonyms, which is not helpful if the coin wants to achieve wider adoption.

Supply wise, there are roughly 72 million OK in existence currently. This number is deliberately larger than some other currencies in order to facilitate micro payments.

Note: OKCash is not to be confused with the Chinese Bitcoin exchange OKCoin.cn - double check any news regarding OKCash

Status (SNT)

Price at Time of Writing - $0.022

Market Cap at Time of Writing - $76,414,847

Available on:

Fiat: BTC9 (CN), b8wang (CN)

BTC: Bittrex, Liqui

Where to store?

Status users ERC20 tokens so can be stored using MyEtherWallet.

Status is an intriguing project that focuses on the mobile space. Based out of Switzerland, it's a free, open source mobile client targeting Android and iOS. The platform itself is built on Ethereum technology. Currently the platform supported 30 languages including Chinese, Korean and Russian. The main focus of the Status project in terms of high level goals is providing a fully private platform, with focus on a lack of censorship and economic transparency.

Co-Founder Jarrad Hope stated "One way to think about Status is that it'll eventually serve as a sort of onramp or gateway so that everyday people can benefit from decentralized applications built on Ethereum, whilst simultaneously helping DApp developers to reach new users."

Status users can search and discover decentralized apps (DApps). Similar to how one would do so on the Apple Store or the Google Play Store on their smartphone now. Examples of these apps include the freelancing platform Ethlance and Ujo, which is a decentralized music licensing and distribution platform. Status definitely have first mover advantage when it comes to a platform like this.

The other main usage here would be a decentralized peer to peer trading market. Similar to how localbitcoins.com currently operates. If Status can provide this for Ethereum based tokens, it could potentially be a game changer for the platform as a whole.

The aim of all this is to provide a digital hub where users only need one identity, as opposed to various usernames, passwords and apps that are common in the current system.

Status also features a built-in messenger with encrypted messaging and the ability to send Ethereum payments between parties, as well as smart contracts. The team chose to focus on messaging first and foremost, as they believed that this was the best and most efficient way to achieve mass market potential. Instant messaging software also has the highest install, and lowest uninstall rate of any mobile software.

The community element is a strong core belief of the platform. Status tokens (SNT) can also be used to ask questions to prominent community members, similar to how one would ask questions on the website Quora. Users can set a minimum number of SNT required to send them a message. This could lead to the rise in "celebrity users" with high levels of SNT required to contact them.

The team also offers rewards for those who can uncover bugs in their code. So far, the team has developed a fully functioning alpha product, with the help of over 6,000 testers.

In terms of competitors,you can think of Whatsapp as being the application with broad similarities to Status. The growth and true potential of Status will depend on the adoption of DApps as a whole, because it's unlikely that it's true calling will be purely as a mass-adopted chat app like Whatsapp or WeChat. If the team can facilitate a DApp store, then there is indeed a lot of room for growth in the coming years. In terms of cryptocurrency based competitors, kik is the one that is likely to be competition to Status in the short term.

One thing to factor with Status, is that first time movers often do not have a long-term advantage. The growth of Status will depend solely on their ability to stay ahead of the market, which is tough when competitors could come in and exploit Status' weaknesses as a platform.

Unlike other cryptocurrency projects, Status was self-funded for the first two years of its life. Supply wise, Status has a total supply of 6 billion, with 41% of this being funds contributed by the public during their July ICO. Interestingly enough, their ICO was designed so that large investments could not dominate the holdings. The Status team actually refunded more ETH than they took in during the ICO period.

The team are very active on their Slack channel (which currently has over 15,000 members), which is something that can't be said for some of the other coins mentioned in this book. Like any complex project, transparency is always a good thing, especially in times when there may not be much to report on the development front.

In terms of roadmap, Status is aiming for a public release towards the end of 2018, or beginning of 2019 - making this a good opportunity to get involved before then. A beta release in the middle of 2018 would give a clearly indication of the long term potential of Status, both as a platform, and as a messaging system.

Tierion (TNT)

Price at Time of Writing - $0.081

Market Cap at Time of Writing - $34,638,811

Available on:

BTC: Liqui, HitBTC (CN),

ETH: EtherDelta

Tierion aims to use blockchain technology as a data verification platform. Using their open source timestamping proof Chainpoint - Tierion has the ability to verify the integrity of a file, record, or process - without having to rely on a third party.

The practical applications for this are widespread. The ability to issue digital receipts for purchases, insurance claims or stock trades, which act as an immutable proof of purchase is a great asset in fighting fraudulent chargebacks and fraudulent transaction claims.

For auditors, the ability to timestamp data with a proof of record will drastically lower the chances for people to go back into a database an alter it. For example, a situation like Enron would not be allowed to happen with data stored on the blockchain. Going one step further, the auditing industry as a whole faces a huge threat from blockchain solution such as Tierion

Medical records, legal records are other areas where blockchain's verification process could have great benefits for society at large in the future.

Many of the above examples are ones that don't just apply to Tierion, but blockchain technology as a whole. That being said - why Tierion?

The answer is simple, speed. Tierion's API lets developers add up to 100 records per second, this is far quicker than previous blockchain solutions. An additional big advantage is their usage of current technology to make the process user friendly. It is much easier to create data stores using HTML forms which are both desktop and mobile compatible, than it is to learn an entire new programming language just for this purpose. This bridge between generations of technology, has great usage potential in the blockchain space for the near future.

Another cool thing about Tierion is its integration with widely used applications such as Salesforce, Gmail, Google Docs, and Mailchimp.

Unlike many of the blockchain based firms in this book, Tierion also has a full functioning product, which you can actually sign up to use for free today. The free version is limited to 15,000 data records per month, which should be more than enough for the average home user. Obviously, from a business standpoint, the money will be made with the Enterprise versions of the software.

The project already has links with some larger multinational companies. An invitation to join Dutch electrical giant Phillips' Blockchain Lab, a thinktank dedicated to see how blockchain technology can be used in healthcare. January 2017 bought an announcement of a working agreement with Microsoft to use blockchain technology to prove data existence and validity.

The big question with Tierion, is the utility of the TNT token itself. Will TNT be adopted as part of the Tierion ecosystem, or will users still prefer to carry that their transactions using a different cryptocurrency.

First Blood (1ST)

Price at Time of Writing - $0.517

Market Cap at Time of Writing - $44,310,766

Available on:

BTC: Bittrex, Liqui

Built on the Ethereum platform and based out of Boston with heavy ties to China, First Blood focuses on the ever growing esports space. First Blood aims to build a blockchain support esports platform that will allow gamers from around the world to compete against one another for prizes.

The use of smart contracts will ensure all results are fair and just, and that no cheating can occur. For those not in the know, the esports world has been plagued by cheating scandals ever since cash prizes were first introduced.

Their marketing efforts have been solid to say the least, and their "from the ground up" marketing strategy includes offering sponsorships to video game live streamers.

In terms of game themselves, First Blood's main focus for now is on the extremely popular Multiplayer Online Battle Arena game DOTA2 - with other game support planned for the future

An already established relationship with blockchain video game developer MOLD was compounded by a huge announcement on October 2nd 2017.

"We are proud to announce we will be working with the Chinese Government and Chinese esports companies to organize esports tournaments!"

More specifically, they're going to be used by the General Administration of Sport of China., the government agency responsible for sports in China. In a statement on their website the team announced

"First Blood will be a partner for hosting the Chinese University Esports League (CUEL). CUEL is a huge competition in China and each year hundreds of thousands of students participate. The partnership with First Blood was put into place as CUEL aimed to reduce their overheard."

The full version of the platform isn't out yet, but previous developer updates have mentioned banning cheaters from the beta platform, which shows that the technology is working at a basic level at least.

Future plans for the coin include support for additional popular games such as League of Legends and Counter Strike: Global Offensive - making this coin one to watch as we move into 2018

2Give (2GIVE)

Price at Time of Writing - $0.0053

Market Cap at Time of Writing - $2,786,042

Available on:

BTC: YoBit, Bittrex

Where to store?

The 2Give team currently has desktop wallets for Windows and Mac available on their website. A Linux wallet is coming soon.

2Give (or GiveCoin 2.0) is a comparatively tiny project when compared to some of the larger ones discussed here like Bytom and Status. With a market cap of just under $3 million dollars, it's safe to say that this one is a long shot indeed, but it's one with a good cause at heart, which is why it made the cut for this book.

From the official website "2GIVE makes it easy to support your favorite non-profit or pro-social cause and can be used for "repaying it forward" through social tipping!" The coin is supported by the Strength in Numbers Foundation, a non-profit digital trust. The idea is that user can donate to their charity of choice, without giving a significant portion of the funds to a payment process, while simultaneously revealing their online identity.

As previously mentioned, 2Give is the newer version of what was known as GiveCoin. The reason for the switch is that GiveCoin suffered from "pool hoppers", miners who switched between mining chains because it was financially advantageous to do so. This led to a system where the top 2% of GiveCoin miners took home most of the mining profits. 2Give's switch to a Proof of Stake model allows fairness to be restored among the mining community.

2Give attracts miners with a social conscience with their reward system, which offers a 5% to miners and stakeholders who help keep the platform operational. Miners then get an additional 1% as a transaction fee for processing payments on the 2Give network.

Many online rumors are flying around regarding 2Give's partnership with a number of large companies, including online streaming service Twitch and even UNICEF. It should be noted that with a market cap as small as this, these rumors can and do have a significant effect on the price.

2Give has received some early adoption, including a partnership with the Japanese Bitcoin ATM network coinoutlet. Coinoutlet ATM users can now buy 2Give at any of the ATM's around the country.

Future plans for the coin include mobile wallets for both iOS and Android, as well as a real world "air drop" in which gift cards will be left in various location to spread awareness of 2Give. The growth of 2Give will be determined largely by the adoption of the idea from non-profits around the world. If larger ones do get involved, then 2Give tokens will therefore have more utility and increase in price accordingly.

Conclusion

Well there we have it. 12 altcoins under $1 that have HUGE potential for gains in the next 12-18 months.

I hope this information has been beneficial to you and has given you a foundation to invest some of the more unknown cryptocurrencies. There has never been a more exciting time for cryptocurrencies than right now, so there's no better time to get involved.

I encourage you to do additional research before investing in any of these, particularly by checking out the white papers on the individual coin websites, which will give you a much more in-depth look at the technology behind them.

Remember to invest wisely (with your own money), don't check your investments on a daily basis, and don't panic sell if you see a dip in the market.

I wish you the best of luck in the cryptocurrency market, and I hope you make a lot of money.

Thanks,

Stephen

Cryptocurrency: Insider Secrets 2

By Stephen Satoshi

Introduction - The Current State of the Cryptocurrency Market

Well, there's never a dull day in the crypto market and the start to 2018 has been no exception. We've seen record highs hit in December and January for a number of coins. Bitcoin reached $19,800, Ethereum topped $1,000 for the first time and Ripple soared to above $3. Since then the news has been more muted, and the market has been moving sideways and downwards for the past couple of months. Now before you think it's all doom and gloom, let's take a few minutes to examine why this movement isn't the worst thing in the world, and what we can expect from the crypto market in the rest of the years.

First of all, we must examine what has been causing the recent price slides. There are a number of reasons for this. The first blow came when it was revealed that a number of credit cards companies were banning users from making cryptocurrency purchases on their cards. This is a step forward as it is in line with other financial instruments. For example, no licensed stock trading website will allow credit card deposits, so crypto applying the same rules is a move in a right direction.

Secondly, we had the federal investigations into Tether, the cryptocurrency that is pegged to the US dollar. In late January, the US Commodity Futures Trading Commision (CTFC) began an investigation into Bitfinex and Tether. Tether claimed that all of its coins were backed by actual US dollars held in reserve, but failed to prove this was the case. Tether nevertheless denied accusations. Bitfinex was dragged into the battle because both companies share the same CEO. This caused the price of crypto to drop as some commentators believed Tethers were being printed to artificially inflate Bitcoin prices. If this is indeed the case, then we as investors should be willing to accept short term losses for a more stable long term market.

The third and final piece of bad news came out of Japan. The Japanese Financial Services Agency fined 7 different cryptocurrency exchanges for not following regulatory rules. The same agency then ordered two other agencies to suspend business altogether. This move came after Tokyo-based firm Coincheck had $530 million worth of cryptocurrency stolen. This news caused the market to drop by 5.3% in a single day. Once again, we should encourage a crackdown on poorly run exchanges if it means long term market stability.

Now, let's get on to the good news. After a senate hearing on cryptocurrency, CFTC chairman Chris Giancarlo made a number of bullish statements on cryptocurrency and blockchain technology. Giancarlo's most poignant line was "We owe it to this new generation to respect their enthusiasm for virtual currencies, with a thoughtful and balanced response, and not a dismissive one." A stance like this from the head of one of the most powerful financial regulatory committees in the US is only going to be a positive - both for consumer and institutional investors. Giancarlo then went onto discussing the benefits of blockchain technology and even discussed the term "HODL" in his speech. Financial regulators will support cryptocurrencies if it means people can make money with them through non-nefarious means. If they have to step in to prevent theft, hacking and use for criminal activity, then so be it.

Speaking on institutional adoption, March brought news of the Coinbase Index Fund. I discuss this later on in this book and what it could mean for crypto going forward, but needless to say, any kind of large scale institutional adoption is only going to be a good thing for cryptocurrency as a whole.

So without further ado, let's move forward and examine some of the best cryptocurrency projects in 2018, and see exactly how you can get involved.

Thanks,

Stephen

10 High Potential Coins Under $1

Ambrosus (AMB)

Price at Time of Writing - $0.55

Market Cap at Time of Writing - $80,288,043

Available on:

BTC: Binance, Kucoin, Livecoin

ETH: Binance, Kucoin, RightBTC

Where to store:

AMB tokens are ERC20 tokens so you can store them in MyEtherWallet or other Ethereum wallets.

Ambrosus is another supply chain cryptocurrency project. This time based out of Switzerland and focused on two main market sectors, namely food and medicine. One of the core technology partners for the Ambrosus project is Parity Technologies.

By using real time sensors, linked to a blockchain, the project promises to monitor the distribution and food and medicine across the entire supply chain network. This will allow for anti-tampering monitoring as well as the enforcement of smart contracts to ensure the product reaches its end destination and an automatic payment is released based on the fulfillment of certain conditions.

For example, if you have a certain food that requires specific temperature, humidity and PH conditions to be met during transportation, a tracking device with a sensor that monitors these would be implemented in the container used to transport the goods. If all conditions are met when it reaches its end destination, then payment would automatically be released. If any of the conditions fail, the recipient would be notified in real time, and thus action could be taken accordingly.

There is also the issue of data storage, a blockchain solution means the data is publicly viewable so there are no issues regarding fraud, data hacking or manipulation.

Ambrosus' main asset at this time is the team behind its development. I would go as far as saying this is the best crypto development for a low market cap coin that I've seen in a long time. Headed up by CEO Angel Versetti, who has a wide industry background including time spent working at the United Nations, where he was the youngest project leader in UN history, and the World Resources Forum. He also has a corporate background with both financial firm Bloomberg and technology giant Google. CTO Dr. Stefan Meyer has a vast supply chain and food industry background having previously led R&D projects at Swiss food giant Nestle. The rest of the team is made up of equal parts storied corporate history and successful blockchain developers. They are backed up with some world class advisors including Oliver Bussman, previously named CTO of The Year by the Wall Street Journal. As well as Prof. Malcolm J W Povey, one of Britain's leading experts in food sensor technology. In a world of fake bio pictures, and develop aliases, a team as open and transparent with a history like this is frankly unprecedented in any but the biggest cryptocurrency projects.

Like many cryptocurrency projects, the Ambrosus project is built using the Ethereum blockchain.

So how is the token valuable? One of the biggest reasons for the low price right now is that the token economics have not yet been finalized. The main usage for AMB will be to facilitate transactions in the Ambrosus network, like how ETH is used for Ethereum and Gas is used for Neo. There are talks of masternodes being available, so users could stake their AMB tokens to help run the network and receive dividends in return. There are current debates about whether there would be larger funds needed to run a node or smaller funds with a legal contract. The alternative for this would be a two tier system with masternodes running alongside peer nodes.

In terms of competitors, there are a number of companies and crypto projects in the supply chain space. Two of the bigger ones out of China are VeChain and WaltonChain. WaltonChain is an RFID centered project, so the two may not be directly comparable. RFID is a limited technology that is pretty much limited to one (albeit important) function. However, with sensor technology, Ambrosus has a much larger usage scope. For example, the ability to monitor temperature and humidity. The project could be compared to Modum in this respect.

Where Ambrosus may be able to win though is the Swiss factor. It is much easier for European companies to do business with a fellow European company than it is for them to deal with Chinese ones. There is also the legitimacy issue. Will a company needing specialized supply chain solutions opt for a partnership with a Swiss company, in a country that has a long standing history of quality and impartiality. Or a Chinese company with a previous history of manipulation, in the case of WaltonChain's fake social media giveaway scandal. Getting first mover advantage and partnerships with large companies is going to be huge in which one of these supply chain projects has the highest ceiling, but Ambrosus certainly has a geographical advantage over its competitors in this respect.

Overall, this is certainly a long-term project with potential industry leading ramifications. As such, I wouldn't expect any giant price movements in the coming months. But as we move forward into 2019, there could well be big things for the Ambrosus project.

Jibrel Network (JNT)

Price at Time of Writing - $0.47

Market Cap at Time of Writing - $71,386,200

Available on:

BTC: Bibox, HitBTC, Gate.io

ETH: Bibox, HitBTC, Gate.io

Where to store:

JNT tokens are ERC20 tokens and thus can be stored using MyEtherWallet or by using a Ledger Nano S.

An interesting project based out of Switzerland that aims to bridge the gap between cryptocurrency and traditional markets. Jibrel focuses on government backed cryptocurrencies, so cryptocurrencies issued by central banks, but that still are backed by blockchain technology. You can think of Jibrel as a "decentral bank" in this respect.

The reason for the project is that while blockchain technology is an incredibly useful innovation, it is still limited in real world implementation due to the lack of widespread adoption for cryptocurrency. Co-Founder Yazan Barghuti summed this up well by saying "People pay their bills, their loans, and their mortgages in dollars, Euros, and pounds. They don't pay them in ETH or BTC."

So by bridging the gap, and implementing smart contracts with non-cryptocurrency based currencies, it will allow optimized real world transactions. For example, if a smart contract had been implemented on sub-prime loans and ratings before the 2008 financial crisis, we could have seen adjustments made prior to the market crash based on the actual performance and makeup of these assets, rather than outside pressure which forced ratings agencies to keep these bonds at a AAA rating. This is just one of the wide ranging theoretical applications of the Jibrel Network project.

Barghuti argues that the end user doesn't necessarily need to know their money is backed by cryptocurrency. They would want to use it the same way they always have. Similar to how online banking doesn't change the currency you are using, it's just backed by a computer instead of a bank book.

How Jibrel plans to do this is by using what it calls CryptoDepository Receipts or CryDRs. This will allow traditional financial assets to be backed by the Jibrel Network's cryptography. So if you held $100 in silver, for example, a USD CryDR would back this up with $100 worth of JNT tokens. These CryDRs could also be used for trading.

As far as the user side of things goes, Jibrel aims to make things simple and this is where the jWallet and jCash make their mark. jWallet will function as a regular cryptocurrency wallet, but aims to bring greater security to the equation. You can also use the wallet to exchange cryptocurrency for fiat currency the same way you would do so on an exchange. This can help protect your assets if you are worried about cryptocurrency volatility.

Initially, the project will run using the Ethereum network. It is interesting to note that all jWallet's will run using Jibrel's own Ethereum nodes, so the end user doesn't have to connect themselves. While some may argue that this is a centralized model, one which cryptocurrency purists often fight against - there are practical implications for this. Barghuti argues that this approach is one that favors scalability more than anything else, stating "'Yeah, but the whole point about Bitcoin is it's off-grid, etc.' Okay you can stay off-grid, and that's a $500 billion market. But if you go on-grid, you can start tackling the issues with the $34 trillion global economy."

Initially, Jibrel will support 6 fiat currencies and 2 further money market instruments, with plans to roll out further currencies in the future. Ultimately it would seem that support for 20 or 30 currencies at the same time would be completely possible.

In terms of the team behind it. Co-Founders Yazan Burghati and Talal Tabbaa both have a strong financial services background, both having previously worked for the Big 4 firms. The technical chops come from Victor Mezrin, who previously ran one of the largest altcoin mining operations in the world.

Going forward, we have the release of the Jibrel institutional level banking platform scheduled for Q3 2018. This will be a big determinant of whether the project is successful or not. There are very few cryptocurrency projects this close to launching such a significant venture, and if it is successful in the early stages, I doubt that Jibrel will stay at its current price. The only competitor coin I can think of who are targeting financial institutions on this scale would be QASH, based out of Japan, who I covered in a previous book.

Then in Q4, the team has planned the full scale launch of the decentralized Jibrel Network. By this time we will have a solid grasp of whether the project is going to be a smash hit, or if it will fall by the wayside. Like any project that deals with banks, licensing is going to be a tricky hurdle to overcome. Different countries have different licensing procedures which take different lengths of time to pass - and we've seen how this can delay projects in the past in the case of debit card projects like Monaco.

Either way, Jibrel Network is an extremely exciting project which huge ramifications if it is successful. A breath of fresh air in the sense that it addresses the current limitations of blockchain technology and aims to give real world application without needing to reinvent the wheel. I wouldn't expect too much price movement in the next quarter, but by the end of the year, we will have a better idea of just how successful the project can be.

LoMoCoin (LMC)

Price at Time of Writing - $0.07

Market Cap at Time of Writing - $18,033,963

Available on:

BTC: Bittrex, CoinExchange

Where to store:

The native LoMo app has a built in cryptocurrency wallet

LoMoCoin, also known as LoMoStar is an intriguing project out of China that focuses on the incentivized shopping space.

First and foremost to truly understand the potential of the coin, you must understand the market it is targeting. Incentivized shopping, in other words, shopping via the use of digital coupons, is a huge deal in China and across Asia. Many businesses have social media accounts, for example on WeChat, China's biggest smartphone social media platform, in which they distribute coupons directly to customers. In other words, if you want to go to Dunkin Donuts, for example, you can follow their WeChat account and you will receive a coupon for doing so. As businesses compete for foot traffic, coupon based shopping is becoming more popular than ever.

The concept centers around the Chinese tradition of "red envelopes". Traditionally these are given out on special occasions like Chinese New Year and contain money. With LoMo, these envelopes would be in the form of discount codes for local stores.

For example, you are out shopping with friends, when suddenly you get a notification on your phone notifying you of a flash sale in a nearby store. This store might even be one of your favorites, and thus you've just scored a huge discount. From the store's perspective, performing airdrops like these builds brand loyalty, and gives them a chance to win new business that they would not previously have had access to.

LoMoStar is the app itself that the currency is distributed through. The app promises to be an all-in-one shopping and social platform where users can not only claim rewards and spend their cryptocurrency, but also perform their own airdrops with their friends. The app also has a built in cryptocurrency exchange, which while not revolutionary, will be convenience once increased adoption continues.

This kind of native advertising brings disruption to the traditional model of sponsored ads like Google AdWords and Facebook Ads. Year by year these are representing lower returns for those using them, as ad price increases and customers get more and more "overmarketed". In other words, they make a lot of money for Google and Facebook, but often represent poor ROI for the businesses running the ads.

The main driving force behind LoMo is the number of users downloading the app itself. As the user base becomes bigger, more businesses have incentives to do airdrops, and thus we can see somewhat of a snowball effect. Having a low barrier to entry "on-ramp" so to speak is a great way to attract those who are new to the cryptocurrency space. We have seen this in the past with coins like Ripple that became "accessible" due to their low price, despite their high market cap and limited room for growth going forward. Being able to take your first step into the crypto world just by downloading a smartphone app is a very simple solution for many users. Especially in target areas like Shanghai as well as other large Asian cities like Tokyo and Seoul.

Many users have reported earning over $100 USD worth of coins within the first few months of having the app on their phones. Which isn't bad seeing as you don't really have to do anything to get them. You can then transfer these tokens to more established cryptocurrencies like Bitcoin and Ethereum if you wish. Once again, this just reiterates the low barrier to entry effect and how this could be a huge bonus going forward.

The big question with this project is the same question we have with any project based in China. There is a certain risk involved with Chinese companies due to the cultural and regulatory differences when compared to the West. This is then compounded by the Chinese government's reactionary stance on cryptocurrency and often sweeping change in the law. For example, one of the biggest events in 2017 was when the government decided that Chinese citizens could not participate in ICOs, which led to a big downturn in the market. What further compounded this drop is that many media outlets in the West reported this event as "China bans cryptocurrency."

In terms of the team, I have to say I was very impressed. There are over 70 employees, many of whom have a solid blockchain background. CEO Xiong LiJian was previously involved in Litecoin mining development on both the hardware and software side.

Then we have to examine the potential for the project outside of China. Although the app currently has airdrops in multiple countries, it remains to be seen just how widespread adoption will be outside of the Middle Kingdom. That said, even if the idea is *only* successful within China, there will still be significant growth from the current price.

Overall, I like the idea of LoMo and their app. The social element could play a big part in bringing new users into the cryptocurrency space, which is vital if the technology is going to grow as we move forward. Low barriers to entry combined with incentivized rewards for using it, mean we could see industry changing ramifications. These are still early days, but if you are interested and want to see for yourself just how the project works, I recommend downloading the app on your iPhone or Android and check it out. After all, if you aren't yet invested in crypto, this could be your first chance to own coins of your very own, without having to invest a single penny.

WePower (WPR)

Price at Time of Writing - $0.17

Market Cap at Time of Writing - $60,534,439

Available on:

BTC: Huobi, Liqui

ETH: Huobi, Liqui

Where to store:

WePower is an ERC20 token and can by stored in MyEtherWallet

An eco-friendly blockchain solution that focuses on the renewable energy sector. By creating a platform that allows green energy producers to interact with energy investors and green energy consumers, they have an incentive to keep creating renewable energy sources. For consumers, they would be able to purchase energy directly at a rate below the market price due to the lack of need for a middleman such as a government body. The project has already been listed as one of the Top 10 innovative energy initiatives in Europe by Fast Company magazine. The size of the renewable energy sector is growing every year with an estimated $200 billion of new investment annually. The team estimates the token market potential to be approximately $1.2 trillion per year.

By using blockchain technology and smart contract implementation, the project solves compliance issues such as a green energy owner selling energy that isn't theirs for example.

The tokens themselves will be tied to energy prices, and thus will naturally be more stable than other cryptocurrencies. This is important when we ask the question of "why can't the project just use BTC or ETH for transactions". By running the platform like this, it gives an inherent need for the WPR token and thus the WPR token itself has an intrinsic value, which is a big part of any cryptocurrency project.

The platform will use an auction model, in which producers put their tokens up for sale and buyers have 48 hours to bid on them. After these 48 hours have expired, non-token holders have the opportunity to buy them as well. This unique approach to trading green energy gives WePower a huge first mover advantage when it comes to the energy trading sector, particularly in the eco-friendly part of it.

The project's initial focus will be on the European market because EU member states all share a common energy agreement with regards to regulations. This agreement makes cross border energy trading relatively seamless. The project is currently in talks with the Lithuanian government about a joint venture with nationalized energy companies. Pilot projects are also underway in Estonia.

The renewable energy sector is one that continues to receive a lot of government support, for both blockchain and non-blockchain ventures. This support could be huge for WePower when we compare it to other cryptocurrencies projects that often run into red tape and bureaucracy. Having backing from a government, rather than having to fight it, will be vital if the project is to succeed.

In terms of the team behind the project, Co-Founder Nikolaj Martyniuk has over 10 years experience in the green energy sector. He is backed up by team members with FinTech backgrounds, energy consultants and blockchain experts.

Progress has been solid so far and a demo platform is already available on the WePower website for users to test out.

A big step for the project came in late February 2018 when it was announced that Binance included WePower in the latest round of voting for inclusion on the platform. This is a community poll where Binance members can vote on coins they want to see included on the platform. If the coin wins the poll then it will be included on Binance for trading. Early results indicate that the coin has been doing well in the polls and at the time of writing ranked number 2 behind Dentacoin.

Going forward, there are a number of near future dates on the roadmap that you need to be aware of. April 2018 will see a full scale testing of the project in Estonia, if this is successful then it will no doubt mean big things for the project. Especially in a space where many crypto projects are still firmly in the theoretical stage. Later testing is scheduled for Q4 2018 in Spain and Australia. The first actual distributed energy will be in December 2018. Then there are further expansion plans for 2019.

Overall, I like the approach of the project with the token system being particularly appealing. The idea of a green energy trading platform without middlemen is a fantastic application of blockchain technology. The need for the WPR token is another huge plus that just can't be overlooked. Listing on a larger exchange will be key in the short term, but the real challenge will be seeing if the testing phases in Estonia, Spain and Australia are successful. If they are, then this coin won't stay this low for long.

TheKey (TKY)

Price at Time of Writing - $0.0187

Market Cap at Time of Writing - Currently unknown due to lack of concrete information about circulating market supply. Based on estimated supply of 3.63 billion, we can make an approximate market cap estimation of around $65,000,000.

Available on:

BTC: Kucoin

ETH: Kucoin

NEO: Kucoin

Where to store:

TheKey uses the Neo protocol (NEP5) and thus you can store it in a Neo wallet. You can download one from the official Neo website https://neo.org/download - desktop, mobile and web wallets are available

Another project coming out of China, TheKey aims to use blockchain technology to create a decentralized national identification system.

This has many different uses in practical terms. One of the main ones being in healthcare. For example, individual citizens could apply for a smart identification card which would be linked to their cellphone. They could then use this to book doctor's appointments online. When they arrive at the hospital, the doctor could have automatic access to their medical records, and their insurance details. The ID could also be linked to a payment method, which could automatically pay for any medical bills required.

This then has anti-fraud ramifications, which could be useful for things like automatically ordering medication. For example, elderly patients could have medicine delivered to their home, so they wouldn't have to leave the house in order to get necessary medicines. Currently, there is no system in place which allows them to do this, because of concerns about people stealing identities to order medicine in order to resell it on the black market.

One of the first ICOs to use the Neo platform rather than Ethereum. ONCHAIN, the company behind Neo is also listed as a strategic partner for the project. The ICO itself was not without problems, as it went live at 2AM CET, which was immediately followed by a website crash and the donation amounts being filled without any chance for European investors to take part.

The coin boasts a number of big partnerships with Chinese companies, namely AliPay (AliBaba's payment platform). There are also plans to trial the technology in two pilot cities, with Jiaxing being the first one.

15 different patents have already been awarded by the Chinese State Intellectual Property Office (SIPO) which is promising to see and shows that the project clearly aims to have a larger scope than others.

The project is headed up by Catherine Li, who boasts an incredibly strong track record of entrepreneurship within China. In 2017 she was awarded Most Outstanding Women Entrepreneurs in China by the All-China Women's Federation. She previously worked at IMS Health, which provides big data solutions in the healthcare space. She is backed up by blockchain lead Ken Huang who worked at phone manufacturer Huawei as a Chief Blockchain Developer.

In terms of competition, the biggest project would be Civic. However, TheKey's focus on China is what makes it stand out. Chinese governments tend to favor internal projects rather than international ones. And if TheKey can garner some early adoption within China, this will make any nationwide or international rollout much easier. This is what sets it apart from the other identity verification blockchain projects. The other factor to remember, especially for a project like this, is that there doesn't only have to be "one winner", many competing projects can and will co-exist side by side, and take up a decent market share.

In terms of roadmap, the project mainnet is scheduled for release in December of 2018.

Right now the low price can be attributed to overall market conditions and lack of listing on a larger exchange. Kucoin is fairly solid and reliable but there just isn't the volume of a Binance or a Bittrex to support higher prices. A March announcement that the coin would be listed on Chinese exchange LBank, which is currently the 16th largest exchange in the world by volume, so this could have some additional growth effects in the short term.

The other drawback is the lack of literature available about the project in English. After studying the official website for some time, I still had a number of unanswered questions that I had to go to unofficial sources within the community to find the answers to. Once greater clarification is made in English on the official website, I have no doubt that more investors will be attracted to the project.

Out of all the projects I've discussed in this book, I'd say this is no doubt one of the more high-risk, high-reward type projects. The Chinese factor, and lack of English communication does mean we could all be mislead into believing the project is further along than it is. However, if you are willing to accept this, this could well be one of the biggest gainers of 2018 and beyond. From a blockchain enthusiast standpoint, it's interesting to see how scalable a NEP5 token will be when compared to one running on the Ethereum network. If TheKey fits your risk/reward profile then it is definitely a project worth checking out.

Note: The project is not to be confused with KeyCoin or SelfKey, which both use the (KEY) symbol. SelfKey in particular focuses on the same space so please ensure you are buying the correct token.

Oyster Pearl (PRL)

Price at Time of Writing - $0.97

Market Cap at Time of Writing - $72,546,189

Available on:

BTC: Kucoin, Cryptopia

ETH: Kucoin, CoinExchange, IDEX

NEO: Kucoin

Where to store:

PRL Tokens can be stored in MyEtherWallet. To create a custom token take the following steps.

Contract Address: 0x1844b21593262668B7248d0f57a220CaaBA46ab9

Symbol: PRL

Decimals: 18

Oyster Pearl addresses the issue of advertising on websites and provides a solution that satisfies both business owners and consumers who are browsing the websites. In their own words "Goodbye banner ads. Hello Oyster." The project combines decentralized storage and payment for content creators.

Currently, it is estimated that 50% of web users have some sort of ad blocking software installed on their computer or on their browser. Much of the other 50% have become somewhat immune to ads due to their frequency.

How it works is by using web visitors' excess computing power (CPU and GPU power) to store files on a decentralized ledger. This excess power provides Proof of Work which maintains the storage network. Site owners are then paid by the storage users, and in turn, web visitors get an ad-free browser experience.

The files themselves are stored on the IOTA tangle and uses Ethereum smart contracts in order to verify correct storage data. Because of all the data is encrypted and decentralized, fragments of files are stored rather than complete ones, this makes the files more secure than if they were stored on a centralized server like Dropbox for example. This model is open source, so the community can monitor it and ensure there is no nefarious action occurring at any time.

The project makes it extremely simple for businesses to adopt. In fact, all you need to do is add a single line of HTML code to your existing website. So any website that can run Javascript, can run the Oyster protocol. In theory, this should also provide little to no browser slow down or impacted computer performance on the user end either. This simplicity is quite remarkable in a space where many blockchain projects require developers to learn entirely new programming languages just to take advantage of a particular project.

There are a number of blockchain cloud storage projects, with a chief competitor being Storj, which is built entirely on the Ethereum blockchain. However, the main difference between the two is that Storj is strictly focused on storage, without the advertising incentives given to website owners. Siacoin is another competitor, although that project has run into numerous difficulties since their ICO last year. Oyster also has no plans to charge fees for downloading any stored files, whereas Sia does charge per download.

The team is headed up by anonymous developer Bruno Block. This person's anonymity is a cause for concern for some investors, while others are less worried about it. I should say that developers wishing to remain anonymous, while strange, is not uncommon in the crypto space. Much of the other team has come forward with their identities, and maintain public LinkedIn profiles. CTO Alex Firmani has a solid background in the cloud storage space, so industry experience is there. Many of the engineers on the project also have active GitHub profiles which is promising to see.

The main areas to monitor going forward are adoption. Will websites actually use the Oyster protocol versus the traditional advertising models like Google AdSense? Another area of caution would be whether the code added to the HTML will flag a site a malicious by certain anti-virus and anti-malware software.

A more technical concern would be the scalability of IOTA's Tangle network, which at this point has yet to be tested. The Oyster team have already said they will move to their own blockchain solution if the Tangle cannot live up to their needs. This is fine in theory, however, in practice, any switch will have a significant impact on the project.

In terms of roadmap, the team are currently in the Testnet A stage of thins, with Testnet B scheduled for later this year. Testnet B will be a public testnet. Mainnet is currently scheduled for April 2018 which is when Oyster will be fully up and running, and tweaks can be made if necessary.

Oyster Pearl tokens (PRL) are ERC20 tokens. After the latest coin burn there are around 98 million tokens in circulation. The token will be used to pay website owners who install the Oyster code on their site.

If you can overlook an anonymous figure heading the project up, Oyster Pearl is an ambitious project with great potential. Seeing a project running on IOTA's tangle is great to see from an adoption standpoint, and this is certainly a coin to look at closely.

ChainLink (LINK)

Price at Time of Writing - $0.51

Market Cap at Time of Writing - $179,183,250

Available on:

BTC: Binance, Huobi, OKEx

ETH: Binance, Huobi, OKEx

Where to store:

LINK tokens are ERC 20 tokens and can by stored on MyEtherWallet or other Ethereum wallets.

Based out of the US, ChainLink is one of the more ambitious projects out there and aims to create a platform where users can attach smart contracts to existing apps and data. This acts as a bridge between non-blockchain resources like bank accounts and data services and a public smart contract ledger. This would allow users to create contracts that perform the same function as real world binding agreements, but without the expensive middleman.

The entire theory behind the project is that current smart contract platform does not function with off-chain resources. Therefore a bridge is needed and that's where ChainLink comes into play. By acting as a bridge, the contract can be verified on the blockchain, without the data feeds needing to be on that blockchain as well.

In terms of use cases, there are many. For example, say you own a large warehouse that stores valuable goods. These goods are stolen one night, and you need to make an insurance claim. However, the insurance company is pushing back by claiming that the magnetic doors to the warehouse may not have been locked and thus this represents user error. By using ChainLink to connect the monitoring data for the doors, with your insurance contract - you would have an undisputed answer to the question. The same goes for an issue like a payment for a delayed flight, using ChainLink you have publicly verifiable data about how late the flight arrived and for what reason.

Maybe the biggest real world use case is in financial reporting. This could be anything from bond rates, interest rates and other derivatives. ChainLink would allow users to connect to external networks (like Bloomberg) in order to verify the correct data and thus the contract would pay out accordingly.

One of the bigger factors ChainLink has going for it is the ability to let users settle contracts in both fiat currency and LINK tokens. This will no doubt help real world adoption of the technology. The team even discusses this on their website and states that the current limitation of other smart contract platforms to mimic real-world financial agreements. As we saw int he case of the Jibrel Network, in the short to medium term, we will need some sort of bridging between traditional finance and cryptocurrency before we see widespread adoption of cryptocurrency only platforms.

The platform currently has partnerships in place with a number of other smart contract firms including zeppelin_os which powers over $1.5 billion worth of smart contracts. Another agreement is in place with Cornell University's Town Crier initiative - a patent pending system which verifies the security and trustworthiness of data.

An agreement is also in place with the payment network SWIFT. This came after the team won the Innotribe Industry Challenge in 2016. They are now working with SWIFT to develop a Proof of Concept - this will be centered around LINK smart contracts verified interest rates across data sources in order to generate a LIBOR average rate. The smart contract will then be used to generate secure payments based on this rate.

The main things holding back the project right now are the small development team. For the first 3 years of the project, there were only two developers, although CEO Sergey Nazarov confirmed at the end of 2017 that they had hired more members. Lack of updates from the team has been an issue, and a lack of public roadmap is also a cause for concern. For a project as mature as this one, greater public visibility is needed in the short term to reassure investors that everything is moving forward as they would have hoped.

In terms of the token itself. There are 1 billion LINK tokens in circulation, of which 350 million are in the current circulating supply. The team holds 30% with the other 70% split between Node Operators (needed to upkeep the network) and the general public. One interesting thing to note is that unlike other projects, there is no minimum staking requirement to become a node operator. Therefore this allows any users to participate in the network and earns passive income for doing so. Although the payout structure is yet to be finalized, this is certainly something to be aware of if you are interested in staking coins but don't have a huge amount of them.

Overall, ChainLink is a solid project that has proven real world application already.The partnerships in place are impressive, and the only thing holding it back is lack of transparency from the team. I would like to see them hire a full time press officer and marketing manager in order to better communicate the progress going forward. However, the technology alone makes this project well worth looking into.

SONM (SNM)

Price at Time of Writing - $0.15

Market Cap at Time of Writing - $54,959,826

Available on:

BTC: Binance, Tidex, Liqui

ETH: Binance, Liqui, Kucoin

Where to store:

SNM tokens are ERC 20 tokens and can by stored on MyEtherWallet or other Ethereum wallets.

SONM is a fascinating supercomputer project powered by the Ethereum blockchain, powered by miners using their idle computer resources. The project has already received some decent mainstream media attention and was voted #6 on the Top 10 Blockchain Projects To Watch Out For in 2018 by EntreprenEuros Magazine.

This has tremendous application including everything from web hosting to mobile and web applications, machine learning, scientific research, servers for hosting video games and video streaming.

This represents advantages to those needing to use these services when compared to the standard centralized solutions that we see today. Because the rental time on the supercomputer is completely flexible with no minimum amounts or minimum contract lengths - buyers only pay for the exact amount they need to use. If the task then takes fewer resources than the buyer anticipated, they will be refunded for the resources they did not need.

Miners have an incentive for powering the network as they will be paid in SNM tokens. You don't have to have a super powerful computer either, you can use your regular desktop or laptop. You can even use other devices with internet capabilities like your XBox and even your cellphone. Originally there were plans for SNM token holders to be rewarded with the network fees from the project, although this was dismissed due to potential regulatory issues (as the token would then be deemed a "security" by the SEC). There are still plans to reward token holders, but the economics have yet to be finalized. This isn't a major issue at this early stage, but it would be nice to see some additional information about this from the team within the next 6 months.

The project can be looked at as similar to Golem (GNT) which I discussed in the first edition of Cryptocurrency: Insider Secrets. Both aim to use idle computer resources to power supercomputers and thus we can view them as direct competitors. The one advantage SONM does have is that it plans to use the supercomputer for a wider variety of applications than just GPU rendering like the Golem project. In terms of development, SONM also has the advantage being further ahead on its roadmap. Once again, we should restate that there's no reason these two projects can co-exist with equal market shares.

Both projects share the same growing pains, namely, can the Ethereum network handle the sheer volume of transactions required to run a supercomputer like this. SONM's solution is to build their own sidechain (essentially an additional blockchain) which will process some of the transactions and lower the overall load on the Ethereum network. This sidechain will reduce all internal transaction costs to zero.

SONM has already announced a partnership with fellow Ethereum project Storj (discussed in Ethereum: Beginners Bible), the decentralized cloud storage platform. This will allow users to share files on the SONM platform. This additional step towards fully decentralized cloud computing is certainly an achievement going forward. Plus, it is always good to see blockchain project working together in order to gain mainstream adoption.

March brought news of another partnership, this time with blockchain AI platform DBrain. DBrain will be utilizing SONM's supercomputer to convert raw data into real world AI solutions for businesses around the world. SONM CEO Alexei Antonov stated, "Collaboration with Dbrain is an excellent way of demonstrating the possibilities of our project."

One thing SONM does extremely well is hitting their roadmap deadlines. From my research, I found they consistently hit project advancements on or before they were scheduled to. This demonstrates consistency from the team, and adds an extra layer of trustworthiness that other cryptocurrency projects simply do not have. Trust is vital in a space where the early years were dominated by news of theft, hackings and criminal activity.

As previously mentioned, users can buying resources using the SNM token, and those donating their idle computing power will be paid using the token as well. This already gives the token an intrinsic value, and use case - which is always one thing to look for when examining cryptocurrency projects.

In terms of roadmap, an MVP was released in late 2017 and a successful bug bounty round (rewarding users for finding bugs or errors in the code) occurred after that. A Windows client was also launched around this time. The first fee payouts are scheduled for Q2 2018. Followed by a full network release along with the full version of the SONM wallet on the Ethereum network - which is scheduled for July-August 2018.

In the short term, continued announcements of collaborations with other companies will be key to driving price action. In terms of growth potential, Golem currently has a market cap 6X higher than SONM's, and while the project is more mature, it seems that the SONM team are moving forward at a faster rate. This is one of the projects in the book that could have significant price action on both a short and long term basis.

OriginTrail (TRAC)

Price at Time of Writing - $0.18

Market Cap at Time of Writing - $48,535,364

Available on:

ETH: IDEx, HitBTC, ForkDelta

Where to store:

TRAC tokens are ERC 20 tokens and can by stored in MyEtherWallet and other Ethereum wallets.

OriginTrail is a blockchain project that focuses on the supply chain sector. The project was developed in order to combat the scalability problems that other decentralized supply chain projects are facing. The project has already won a number of plaudits in the industry including Walmart China's Food Safety Innovation and the Food + City People's Choice Award.

Supply chain data is often fragmented, as it comes from multiple different sources. This makes it difficult to track and monitor. OriginTrail aims to make this data more manageable without slowing down the process. You could potentially use this to track foos deliveries and authenticity of products when looking at their labels among other things. For example, a 2017 study showed to 70% of wine sold in China was fake. Meaning that it's origins were not what was stated on the bottle and was instead a mix of cheaper wine and water. This fake wine is then sold at a huge markup, which is often over 1000%. There have also been stories of rice contamination across the country. Another investigation, this time by the Wall Street Journal indicated that over one third of the fish sold in the United States was mislabeled. Needless to say, the current solutions are not offering the level of transparency that consumers require.

One very important thing to note is that the OriginTrail network can function across different blockchain protocols. This is known in the industry as being "blockchain agnostic". So it can be used in conjunction with projects built on Ethereum, Neo and IOTA for example, rather than just being limited to one of these at a time. This cross-operability is a huge step in any blockchain project, let alone one that has a lot of potential adoption like the supply chain sector. This would also allow large institutions (like Walmart for example) to build their own blockchain solutions and OriginTrail would be compatible with these. This could also potentially lead to partnerships with some of the biggest players in the industry.

This has many different applications across the sector including product authentication, supply chain management and food journey visibility. As well as backend functions like inventory management and production alert systems.

This is not a new initiative, and the core team has been performing supply chain tracing since 2013. However, they only began implementing blockchain technology in 2016.

The coin is backed up by a solid development team, each with a visible public profile on LinkedIn and extensive industry experience. Co-Founders Tomaz Levak and Ziga Drev both having backgrounds in supply chain management and tracing supply chains in Eurosope and the Middle East.

In terms of token use, TRAC tokens are a necessity for the network to function. The tokens are used to create nodes that hold up the network and process data transactions. Those who run nodes will be rewarded in the form of TRAC tokens. It is not yet confirmed if the project will use masternodes, and if so, how much these will be. Nor has any potential reward amount been confirmed yet. If you do have enough TRAC tokens to run a masternode, this would represent a fantastic passive income opportunity.

In terms of roadmap, the beta version of the testnet is currently scheduled for June. This will be the iron out any kinks and test OriginTrail's applications in various environments. After this, the mainnet is planned for Q3 2018 release.

Lack of a big exchange is the big thing holding back the price as of now. Not only are they not on the bigger exchanges like Binance or Bittrex, there aren't even any coin pairings on an exchange I would consider "mid-level" at this point.

OriginTrail is one of those cryptocurrency projects with industry changing ramifications IF they can achieve widespread adoption. It's a big if, as supply chain management is arguably the most competitive of the cryptocurrency project niches. However, their blockchain agnostic design may well be the "killer application" of this particular project. The ability to work with both open source and private blockchains is simply too be to be ignored, and thus this makes OriginTrail a project well worth looking into.

Note: BTC/TRAC trading is available on CoinFalcon (not to be confused with scam crypto lending platform Falcon Coin) - but the volume available is so low (<$1000 daily) I have not formally included it

Mercury Protocol (GMT)

Price at Time of Writing - $0.02

Market Cap at Time of Writing - $4,420,198

Available on:

ETH: ForkDelta

Where to store:

GMT tokens are ERC 20 tokens and can be stored in MyEtherWallet and other Ethereum wallets

By far the smallest crypto project discussed in this book, with a market cap of just under $4.5 million, Mercury Protocol is a decentralized communication platform. The project itself has been around for over 4 years, with blockchain implementation starting in 2016. On the website, Mercury Protocol lists famed billionaire Mark Cuban as an advisor. Cuban is an investor in Radical App LLC, the parent company behind the project.

The reasoning behind the project is that the current messaging model is centralized and relies on selling user data to advertisers for profit.

The platform offers demographic targeting as well, so advertisers can focus in on their audience, without wasting money by sending announcements to those who are not interested in what they are selling.

The main question you may be asking yourself at this point is - why would someone use Mercury Protocol built apps over other messaging apps that have their own internal economy such as WeChat? The answer to this is that GMT tokens are transferable across different Mercury Protocol apps. The theory behind this is that by allowing use across multiple platforms, it will create a network effect that will expand the user base and encourage widespread adoption. To give an example, imagine if there was a single token you could use on Facebook, Instagram, Whatsapp and Slack - this would be rather handy for both advertisers and users alike.

There are plans to make the entire platform open source in future released, so developers may then be able to make modifications and find any code bugs. There are concerns that this would lead to the rise of "clone platforms" - however, any clone platforms would need a large user base themselves to benefit from this.

GMT or Global Messaging Tokens can be used by network providers to make announcements on the network. The wider audience you want to make an announcement to, the more tokens it will cost. Users could be rewarded with tokens for watching adverts as well, which encourages them to use the platform in the first place. The team also believes that these tokens can incentivize good behavior on the platform and be used to eliminate trolling and online bullying. For example, users will be deducted tokens for harassment. The use of GMT versus BTC or ETH was done to minimize volatility from external factors. For example, if you buy a premium message with 1 ETH, then the price of ETH rises because of unrelated news, then you have just lost out. By using GMT, the price is generally only affected by activity within the Mercury Protocol network.

The token supply is fixed, so there is no mining involved. Users can earn more tokens by participating in the apps themselves.

In terms of roadmap, the mainnet release of the Dust app, the first built on the protocol, is scheduled for Q1 2018. You can download the beta version right now from the App Store or Google Play Store if you want to check it out for yourself. A second app known as Broadcast is currently in development.

The primary concern right now is the complete lack of any marketing effort from the core team. I understand they are working hard on the platform itself, but personally I believe that a coin should always be marketing itself, at least in order to stay relevant in a space that sees multiple projects pop up every day. Even a small weekly update on development progress would be a start. Once we move further into 2018, then talks of partnerships can be discussed and moved along.

In summary, this is no doubt a high risk project because of the small size and need for mass adoption to be successful. I think that it may see more success in niche markets rather than a full on social media 2.0 vision that some share. Even with niche market success though, there's no doubt the current token price and market cap would rise. They have a working product out which is a plus as well. All in all, for the low barrier to entry, it's a solid project with a lot of room to grow and should be looked at closely.

How to Buy Coins on Coinbase With Zero Transaction Fees

Please note: This method only works for countries eligible for Revolut bank accounts which include the USA, Canada and the UK.

If you haven't heard of Revolut, it's a digital bank based in the UK. There have free currency transfers among 26 currencies - which is how we can use this to our benefit. You can even open an account in less than 30 seconds by using the Revolut app.

This is beneficial for Coinbase users because you can save up to 4% on each transaction by doing this, so if you're heavily involved in crypto you can potentially save hundreds of dollars per year.

Now, onto how Revolut can help you save money on cryptocurrency transactions.

Step 1: Send your native currency like GBP or USD, to your Revolut account via debit card. This step is easy and Revolut walks you through it when you set up an account. This transfer should be near instant.

Step 2: Exchange your native fiat currency to Euros on Revolut. Revolut has no transaction fees for this, so you get the market rate.

Step 3: Bank transfer your Euros from Revolut to Coinbase. This is the only step which is not instant, it takes 1 business day, so if you do it before 3PM EST you should get your coins before 9AM the next morning.

Step 4: Once your Euros are in your Coinbase account, transfer them to your GDAX wallet from Coinbase. If you're not familiar with GDax, it is Coinbase's sister platform designed for traders. Transfer between Coinbase and GDax are instant and free.

Step 5: Buy your coins on GDAX using Euro pairings, making sure to use Limit orders instead of Market orders, as these are free. If you use market orders, you will pay a 0.25% transaction fee.

Step 6: Transfer your newly purchased coins from GDAX to a personal wallet, or another exchange like Binance.

A Brand New Way to Buy Cryptocurrency Which Could Have Huge Market Ramifications

March brought news of an exciting development for those of you who want to get involved in cryptocurrency, but don't want to go through the process of buying and storing coins yourself.

I should note at the outset, this method is not viable for those of you only looking to buy a small amount of coins. This is strictly reserved for this with a lot of cash to spend.

US exchange Coinbase announced that they would be beginning the Coinbase Index Fund, aimed at becoming the "Dow of Cryptocurrencies". The fund will automatically diversify your cryptocurrency portfolio and rebalance it on a monthly basis. In the beginning, the fund will feature Bitcoin, Ethereum, Litecoin and Bitcoin Cash, any new coins added to Coinbase will automatically be added to the fund.

In the beginning stages, the fund will be offered to accredited US investors with assets of more than $1 million. Eventually, the threshold will be lowered in stages until the minimum investment is $10,000. There are also plans to roll the fund out across other geographical markets. The fund will charge a 3% management fee, which on the surface seems high. However, if you are looking for a truly passive crypto asset, this may well tick all your boxes.

How does this benefit the rest of the market? Any kind of institutional adoption is a positive sign. Last year we had 2 different Bitcoin ETFs rejected by the SEC on volatility grounds, so this is the next best option in the interim.

Things You Need to Be Aware of With Certain Cryptocurrency Channels on YouTube

For those of your planning to do extra research before buying coins, which is something I always recommend - YouTube is a great place to start. Many content creators do an in-depth analysis of coins in a similar fashion to what I do here. However, there are certain red flags you should look out for when determining how reliable the information on a certain channel is.

The creator has been paid to advertise coins in the past

Many of these channels, especially the ones with larger followings, are paid by the cryptocurrency teams to advertise the coin on their channel. There is no inherent problem with this, after all, it is just a form of advertising. The problem lies where the creator does not disclose they received payment to discuss the coin. And instead disguises this analysis in the form of a supposedly unbiased review.

The creator uses high pressure sales tactics or fake scarcity

Language such as "this coin will go up any day now" or "get in fast before you miss out", designed to spark a fear of missing out among the viewer, are rife in the crypto space. If a channel discusses a coin's price moreso than the project or team behind it, then you must be skeptical. If you find a channel that does this, then you have to take their "advice" with a pinch of salt.

The creator does not disclose their current holdings

There's nothing wrong with cryptocurrency personalities having their own portfolio, however, they should disclose whether they own a coin or not before discussing it in a public space.

The big one: They make promises of guaranteed returns

This one is the biggest red flag. There is a huge difference between discussing projects with potential and promising guaranteed returns if you invest in a certain project. This often is associated with coin lending platforms, such as BitConnect and Davor Coin, both of which exit scammed and caused anyone invested in them to lost 95% of their money. Remember this moreso than anything else. **There is no such thing as guaranteed returns in any investment - cryptocurrency or otherwise.**

Note: While writing this book, another lending platform Falcon Coin performed an exit scam, leaving investors with 98% losses on their initial investment.

Conclusion

And that's it - 10 more exciting altcoins under $1 that have fantastic potential for gains in the next 12 months and beyond.

I hope this information has been beneficial to you and has given you a foundation to invest some of the more unknown cryptocurrencies. Even with the rocky start to the year, there has never been a more exciting time for cryptocurrencies than right now. Even if you missed the boat with coins like Neo and Stellar, it's not too late.

As always, I encourage you to do additional research before investing in any of these, particularly by checking out the white papers on the individual coin websites, which will give you a much more in-depth look at the technology behind them.

Remember to invest wisely, and always with your own money. Never borrow money to invest in cryptocurrency or anything else. For your own sanity, don't check your investments on a daily basis. This is a volatile market, and you have to be willing to accept that if you are to make long term profits. Perhaps most importantly, don't panic sell if you see a dip in the market. From a personal standpoint, if I had sold during the crash caused by the famous Mt. Gox incident, in which Bitcoin lost over 60% of its value - I would be a much poorer man than I am today.

I wish you the best of luck in the cryptocurrency market, and I hope you make a lot of money.

Thanks,

Stephen